KS2 Success

Age 10-11

Maths

10-Minute Tests

Jason White

Sample page

clear instructional text   topic being covered   test number for quick reference

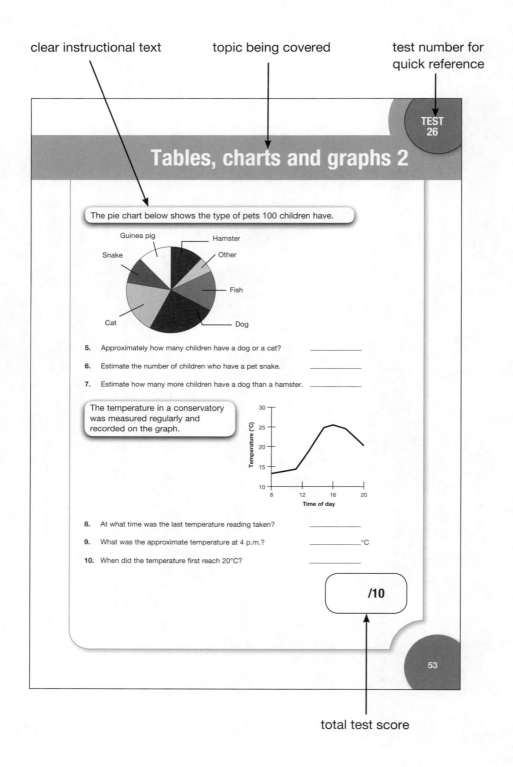

Tables, charts and graphs 2

TEST 26

The pie chart below shows the type of pets 100 children have.

5. Approximately how many children have a dog or a cat? _____

6. Estimate the number of children who have a pet snake. _____

7. Estimate how many more children have a dog than a hamster. _____

The temperature in a conservatory was measured regularly and recorded on the graph.

8. At what time was the last temperature reading taken? _____

9. What was the approximate temperature at 4 p.m.? _____ °C

10. When did the temperature first reach 20°C? _____

/10

53

total test score

Contents

Place value and ordering

1. Put a circle around the largest number below.

   10 358   10 538   (10 835)   10 700   10 799

2. Write in words the value of the digit in bold in each number.

   a) 1289   _two hundred_

   b) 12 289   _two thousand_

   c) 128 952 _twenty thousand_

3. Calculate the following.

   a) 1327 + 72 + 154 = _1553_

   b) 549 + 91 + 3584 = _4224_

   c) 2057 + 1424 + 49 = _3530_

   _1327_
   _154_
   _72_
   _1553_

   _3584_
   _549_
   _91_
   _4224_

   _2057_
   _1424_
   _49_
   _3530_

4. Put these numbers in order, starting with the **smallest**.

   a) 2851   1067   2809   2799   4001

1067	2799	2809	2851	4001

   b) 6430   6515   7000   6001   6099

6001	6099	6430	6515	7000

5. Put these numbers in order, starting with the **largest**.

   a) 12 483   103 826   17 001   1 031 710   87 271

1031710	103826	87271	17001	12483

   b) 4 280 338   583 200   2 984 988   560 200   100 999

4280338	2984988	583200	560200	100999

6. Put these decimals in order, starting with the **smallest**.

   a) 4.2   4.03   4.27   4.09   4.099

4.03	4.09	4.099	4.2	4.27

   b) 20.9   20.72   24.27   20.01   24.4

20.01	20.72	20.9	24.27	24.4

Place value and ordering

$2\frac{1}{3}$ $2\frac{2}{5}$ $3\frac{1}{2}$ $1\frac{1}{9}$ $1\frac{1}{2}$

7. Put these fractions in order, starting with the **largest**.

$\frac{7}{3}$ $\frac{12}{5}$ $\frac{7}{2}$ $\frac{10}{9}$ $\frac{3}{2}$

$\frac{7}{2}$	$7\frac{2}{3}$	$\frac{12}{5}$	$\frac{3}{2}$	$\frac{10}{9}$

8. Six boys from class 4 have their height measured.

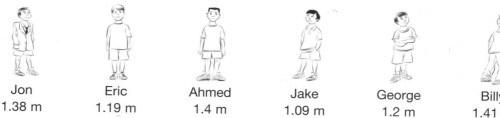

Jon	Eric	Ahmed	Jake	George	Billy
1.38 m	1.19 m	1.4 m	1.09 m	1.2 m	1.41 m

a) Who is the tallest boy?   ~~taht~~ Billy

b) Who is the second smallest boy?   Eric

c) Who is the third tallest boy?   Jon

9. The cost of five train journeys is as follows:

A	Nottingham – Lincoln	£10		**B**	Macclesfield – Stoke	£8.50
C	Carlisle – Manchester	£13.29		**D**	London – Bristol	£24
E	Brighton – London	£16.90				

a) Write the letter of the cheapest journey.   B

b) Write the letter of the second least expensive journey.   A

c) Write the letter of the most expensive journey.   D

10. The total minutes played by a football team's players during a season was as follows.

Player	Minutes played
Johnson	3784
Smith	2072
Adams	4365
Grant	1309
Morgan	1091

a) Which player played the second fewest number of minutes?   Grant

b) Which player played the third most number of minutes?

Smith

/10

Rounding and approximating

1. Round each of these numbers to the **nearest 10**.

   a)   435   367   901   251

440	370	900	250

   b)   6478   7045   8889   5807

6480	7050	8890	5810

   c)   29 837   17 995   21 001   99 507

29 840	~~17 100~~ 18 000	21 000	99 510

2. Round each of these numbers to the **nearest 100**.

   a)   239   965   687   309

200	1000	700	300

   b)   5809   4150   6668   3359

5800	4200	6760	3400

   c)   23 059   57 868   30 951   89 982

23 100	57 900	31 000	80 000

   d)   128 308   451 222   927 010   369 971

128 300	451 200	927 000	370 000

3. Round each of these numbers to the **nearest 1000**.

   a)   560   2506   6444   8099

1000	3000	6000	8000

   b)   11 555   29 537   68 299   37 085

12 000	30 000	68 000	37 000

   c)   222 481   708 564   501 901   199 489

222 000	709 000	502 000	199 000

4. Here are the heights of six children.
   Round each child's height to the nearest 10 cm.

Child 1	Child 2	Child 3	Child 4	Child 5	Child 6
1.24 m	1.31 m	1.2 m	1.41 m	1.33 m	1.49 m

Child 1 = __1.20__ m   Child 2 = __1.30__ m   Child 3 = __1.20__ m

Child 4 = __1.40__ m   Child 5 = __1.30__ m   Child 6 = __1.50__ m

Rounding and approximating

5. Estimate the answers to the questions below and then check your answers with a calculator.

Question	Estimate	Answer
2129 + 3454	5500	
24 783 + 15 031	40000	
7.92 + 15.01	23.00	
5203 – 3487	1500	

6. Estimate how much water is in this jug.

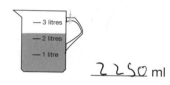

2250 ml

7. Look at these scales and estimate the weight.

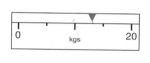

13 kg

8. The boy shown is 123 cm tall. Estimate the height of the woman standing next to him.

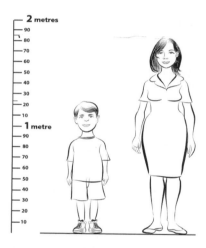

_____ cm

9. Lily can read two pages in her reading book in 4 minutes and 6 seconds. Approximately how long will it take Lily to read 30 pages?

_____ minutes

10. Approximately how many weeks are there in 50 years?

_____ weeks

/10

Number patterns and negative numbers

1. Work out the next two numbers in this sequence.

3	6	12	24	48	96

2. Work out the next two numbers in this sequence.

160	80	40	20	10	5

3. Draw the next two shapes in this sequence.

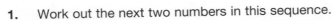

4. Work out the missing number in this sequence.

−14	−8	−2	4	10	16

5. Work out the missing numbers in this sequence.

13	5	−3	−11	−19	−25

6. The temperature in a fridge is −4°C. When the electricity is turned off, the temperature rises by 3°C every hour.

   What is the temperature in the fridge four hours after the electricity is turned off?

    _____ 8 _____ °C

   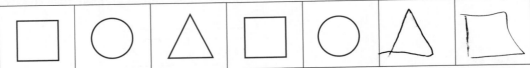

7. A liquid freezes at −16°C. The frozen liquid is heated up by 6°C every 30 minutes.

   What is the temperature of the liquid after two hours of heating?

   _____°C

8. Look at the thermometer.

If the temperature cooled by 18°C, what would be the new reading on the thermometer?

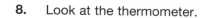 ─4 ~~18~~ _____ °C

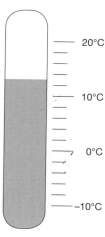

9. Look at the thermometer.

If the temperature increased by 14°C, what would be the new reading on the thermometer?

 6 °C

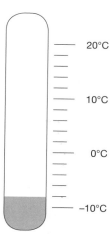

10. A thermometer reads 27°C. If the temperature drops by 3°C every two hours, how long would it take for the temperature to reach −9°C?

_____ 12½ _____ hours

25
22
19
16
13
10
7
5
2
─1
─4
─7
─10

/10

Formulae and equations

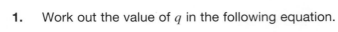
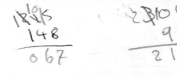

handwritten working: 18 14 5 148 067   2 10 8 92 216

1. Work out the value of q in the following equation.

$215 - q = 148$. $q = \underline{67}$

2. What is the value of z in the equation below?

$z + 92 = 308$ $z = \underline{216}$

handwritten working: 112 32 80

3. $s + t + w = 112$

If $s = 32$ and $t = w$, what is the value of w?

handwritten working:
112
32
80

$32 + 40 + 40 = 112$

32
40
40
112

$w = \underline{40}$

4. There are 146 marbles in a jar. 18 are red, 28 are green and the rest are blue or yellow. There are three times more yellow than blue. Work out the number of blue marbles and the number of yellow marbles.

handwritten working:
18
28
46

0 2 5
4) 100
8
020

25
28
25
75

25
75
100

Blue marbles = $\underline{25}$ Yellow marbles = $\underline{75}$

5. In a cinema there were 200 adults and children. If there was one adult for every three children, how many adults and how many children were there?

Adults = $\underline{50}$

Children = $\underline{150}$

handwritten working:
1:3
050
4) 200
20
00

Formulae and equations

6. a) If $36 - y = x$, what are all the possible values of x that are also a multiple of 4?

32, 28, 24, 20, 16, 12, 8, 4

b) If $28 = zy$, what are all the pairs of whole numbers which satisfy this equation?

7. A rectangle has a perimeter of 54 cm. The lengths of the longest sides are double those of the shortest sides. What are the lengths of the sides?

Shortest = ___6.75___ cm

Longest = ___13.5___ cm

8. A boy is eight years older than his sister. How old is his sister when he is three times older than her?

___2½___

9. $a = 9$, $b = 2a$, $c = b - a$

What is the value of c if a is doubled? $c = $ ___0___

10. $66z = 11y$

If $z = 7$, what is the value of y? $y = $ _____

/10

Decimals

1. Put a circle around the largest decimal below.

   8.02   8.002   (8.2)   8.022   8.020

2. Write in words the value of the digit in bold in each number.

   a)   14.05   _units_

   b)   14.5   _tenth_

   c)   14.005   _hundreds_

3. Double the following decimals.

   a)   0.3   _0.6_

   b)   1.4   _2.8_

   c)   3.82   _7.64_

   d)   0.09   _0.18_

4. Work out the answers to these calculations.

   a)   1.2 x 3 =   _3.6_

   b)   4.08 x 5 =   _20.40_

   c)   6.1 x 7 =   _42.70_

   d)   13.02 x 2 =   _26.04_

5. Work out the answers to these calculations.

   a)   3.8 – 2.2 =   _1.6_

   b)   4.9 + 6.3 =   _11.2_

   c)   18.09 – 4.2 =   _13.89_

   d)   23.6 + 14.23 =   _37.83_

_25.40_
_29.72_
_21.80_
_301.02_
_33.19_
_24.50_
_63.53_

_4.08_

_17 9_
_18.09_
_4.20_
_13.89_

_23.60_
_14.23_
_37.83_

6. Harry has a weekly shopping list. This week he decides to get two weeks' worth of shopping in one go. Write the new amounts Harry must get.

	Old amount	New amount	
Carrots	1200 g	2400	kg
Potatoes	2.5 kg	5	kg
Tomatoes	0.45 kg	0.90	kg
Onions	3	6	
Peas	300 g	600	kg

7. Class 3 did a sponsored walk. They split into six groups and the money they raised was as follows:

Group 1: £13.28   Group 2: £10.50   Group 3: 1571p

Group 4: £8   Group 5: 1108p   Group 6: £12.99

How much money did class 3 raise altogether?   £ 15.71

8. Here are the weights of some children. Work out how much they weigh altogether.

25.4 kg   28.72 kg   21.8 kg   30.02 kg   33.19 kg   24.5 kg   163.53 kg

9. A jug can hold 2,200 ml of water. It takes 100 jugs of water to fill a tank.

How much water can the tank hold if it is full? Give your answer in litres.

____220____ litres   220.000

10. Mary measures her stride. It is 85 cm.   170.00

If Mary takes 200 strides, how many metres has she gone?

____170____ m

/10

Addition

1. Calculate the answer to the following additions. Write the answers as numbers.

   a) Thirteen add fifty-eight = _71_

   b) Seventy-five add thirty-four = _109_

   c) Forty-six add ninety-seven = _143_

2. Add these numbers.

   a) 128 + 308 = _436_

   b) 437 + 292 = _729_

   c) 830 + 405 = _1235_

3. Now work these out.

   a) 45
      +61
      ___
      106

   b) 83
      +39
      ___
      122

   c) 72
      +29
      ___
      101

4. Calculate the additions below.

   a) 1 583
      +8 769
      _____
      10352

   b) 40 147
      + 6 954
      _____
      47161

   c) 28 024
      +79 867
      _____
      107891

5. Add together 14 258, 92 001, 12 119, 85 357 and 48 080.

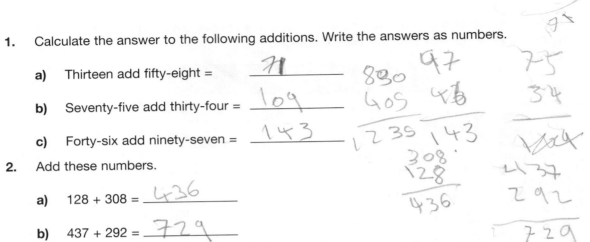

   14258
   92601
   12119
   _____
   118378

   118378
   °85357
   48080
   _____
   251815

   251815

6. Bill goes to the cinema and spends £4.60 to watch a film. He also buys a bag of popcorn which costs £2.75. How much does Bill spend altogether?

   £ _7.35_

   4.60
   2.75
   ____
   7.35

7. Jenny goes shopping and buys a dress, a top and a pair of shoes. Calculate how much money Jenny spends.

Dress	£14.90
Top	£9.99
Shoes	£54.50

£ _7 9.39_

8. How many metres of painting does a groundsman have to complete to mark out all of the lines shown on this netball court?

30 m

16 m

15 m

3 m

```
  60
  60
  32
   3
 ‾‾‾‾
 155
 ‾‾‾‾
```

_155_ m

9. How much money do these three children have altogether?

£ _17.02_

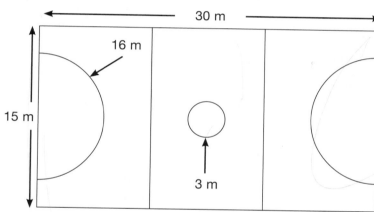

£4.77

£8.43   £3.82

```
 8.43
 4.77
 3.82
‾‾‾‾‾
17.02
‾‾‾‾‾
```

10. Write in the missing digits.

| 8 | 2 | 9 | + | 1 | 6 | 4 | = | 9 | 9 | 3 |

/10

Subtraction

Handwritten working in left margin:

```
 6
7 13
2 7
-----
4 6

4 11
1 8
-----
3 3

5 11
3 5 8
-----
2 1 3
```

```
8 9 14
  3 6
-----
  5 8
```

1. Calculate the answer to the following subtractions. Write the answers as numbers.

   a) Seventy-three subtract twenty-seven = __46__

   b) Ninety-four subtract thirty-six = __58__

   c) Fifty-one subtract eighteen = __33__

2. Calculate these subtractions.

   a) 571 – 358 = __213__

   b) 907 – 668 = __239__

   c) 325 – 179 = __146__

   Handwritten working:
   ```
     8 9 8 17
       6 6 8
     -------
       2 3 9
   ```
   ```
     2 8 8 15
       1 7 9
     -------
       1 4 6
   ```

3. Calculate the subtractions below.

   a)   82
      – 34

        28

   b)   53
      – 37

        16

   c)   61
      – 19

        42

   Handwritten working (right side):
   ```
     6 7 0 0  8 1 2
       9 2 7 4 3
     -----------
     6 0 7 5 6 9
   ```

4. Find the answers to the following subtractions.

   a)   2508
      – 1793

        0715

   b)   92 637
      – 24 081
      ----
        68 556

   c)   700 312
      – 92 743
      ----
        607 569

5. Take away 265 096 from 1 062 884.

   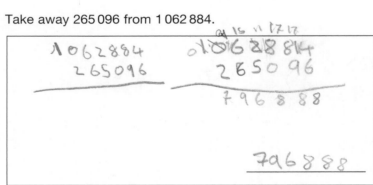

   ```
   1 0 6 2 8 8 4
     2 6 5 0 9 6
   ```
   ```
   0 1 0 6 2 8 8 4
       2 6 5 0 9 6
   -----------------
       7 9 6 8 8 8
   ```

   __796 888__

6. Heather has £20. She spends £12.27 in a shop.

   How much money does she have left?

   £ __7.73__

   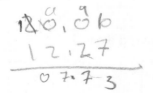

   ```
   1 0 . 0 6
   1 2 . 2 7
   ---------
   0 7 . 7 3
   ```

Subtraction

(handwritten working at top:) 28.8 6 / 26.4 / 03.6

(handwritten working at top right:) 15.06 / 28.90 / 2.50 / 26.40

7. Emily went shopping and spent £8.90 on food, £2.50 on some socks and £15 on a dress. How much money did she have left out of £30?

   £ __3.60__

8. A baker had 6 kg of flour. He needed 225 g of flour to make one cake.

   If he made 12 cakes, how much flour did he have left?

   (handwritten working:)
   225
   12
   450
   2250
   2700

   56000
   2700
   3300

   __3.3__ kg

9. A full tank holds 520 litres of water. The tank is then drained by pulling the plug out.

   40 litres of water drains through the plug hole every minute.

   How many minutes will it take until the tank holds 200 litres?

   (handwritten working:)
   40
   80
   120
   160
   200
   240
   280
   320

   520
   200
   320

   8944
   398
   546

   __8__ minutes

10. Write in the missing digits.

    | 9 | 4 | 4 | — | 3 | 9 | 8 | = | 5 | 4 | 6 |

    /10

Fractions

1. Calculate the answer to the following addition.

$$2\frac{5}{7} + 1\frac{4}{7} =$$

$$\frac{19}{7} + \frac{11}{7} = \frac{30}{14} \qquad \frac{4}{1} \qquad 4\frac{2}{7}$$

2. Write in the missing fraction.

$$\frac{1}{8} + \frac{1}{4} + \boxed{\frac{5}{8}} = 1 \qquad \frac{1}{8} \quad \frac{2}{8} \quad 5$$

3. Calculate the answer to the following subtraction.

$$5\frac{1}{6} - 3\frac{3}{4} =$$

$$\frac{31}{6} - \frac{15}{4} = \qquad \frac{16}{} \qquad \frac{8}{1}$$

4. Calculate the answer to the following subtraction.

$$7\frac{2}{5} - 3\frac{7}{10} =$$

$$\frac{74}{10} - \frac{37}{10} = \frac{37}{10}$$

5. Calculate the answer to the following multiplication.

$$\frac{2}{3} \times \frac{3}{4} =$$

Write the answer in its simplest form.

Fractions

6. Write the answers to the following divisions.

   a) $\frac{1}{3} \div 2 =$

   b) $\frac{3}{4} \div 6 =$

   c) $\frac{1}{4} \div 4 =$

7. Put the following fractions in order, starting with the **smallest**.

   $\frac{12}{3}$ $\frac{19}{5}$ $\frac{3}{2}$ $\frac{29}{8}$ $\frac{13}{6}$

   _____ _____ _____ _____ _____

8. A survey was taken of 30 children's favourite flavour of ice cream. $\frac{2}{5}$ of the children liked strawberry, $\frac{1}{3}$ liked chocolate and the rest liked vanilla. What fraction of the children liked vanilla the best?

9. At a party, a birthday cake was divided into 24 equal pieces. $\frac{3}{8}$ of the cake was eaten straightaway and $\frac{1}{3}$ of the cake was taken home in party bags. What fraction of the cake was left?

10. Calculate $\frac{7}{3} + \frac{1}{4} + \frac{11}{12}$.

    /10

Multiplication

1. Multiply the following numbers by 10, 100 and 1000.

    a) 2.71 x 10 = _____   **b)** 3.09 x 10 = _____   **c)** 46 x 10 = _____
            x 100 = _____   x 100 = _____   x 100 = _____
            x 1000 = _____   x 1000 = _____   x 1000 = _____

2. Calculate the answer to the following multiplication.

    ```
        1742
    x     23
    ```

3. Calculate the answer to the following multiplication.

    ```
        7061
    x     15
    ```

4. Calculate the answer to the following multiplication.

    ```
        5934
    x     61
    ```

5. An electrician earns £1732 every month. How much does she earn in a year?

Multiplication

6. Mr Morgan's newspaper bill is £11.57 each week. How much does Mr Morgan pay in a year?

7. In a box there are 36 watermelons. An average watermelon weighs 1250 g. Calculate the approximate total weight of watermelons in the box.

8. A rugby shirt costs £14.89. The rugby club need 19 shirts for their new team. How much will it cost to buy the 19 shirts?

9. Polly fills a bucket with water. She uses 43 cups of water altogether. Each cup holds 381 ml of water. How much water is there in the full bucket?

10. A fence panel is 1.245 m long. Mr Jones needs 23 panels to enclose his allotment. What is the perimeter of his allotment?

/10

Division

1. Divide the following numbers by 10, 100 and 1000.

    a)   24 ÷ 10 = _____
         ÷ 100 = _____
         ÷ 1000 = _____

    b)   357 ÷ 10 = _____
         ÷ 100 = _____
         ÷ 1000 = _____

    c)   2598 ÷ 10 = _____
         ÷ 100 = _____
         ÷ 1000 = _____

2. Work out the answer to the division below.

    17 | 1394

3. Work out the answer to the division below.

    72 | 2664

4. Work out the answer to the division below.

    28 | 2324

5. A plumber earns £2368 in July. He is paid £16 for every hour that he works. Calculate the number of hours he worked in July.

Division

6. Mrs Williams pays £1404 in a year for her electricity. How much does she need to save each week to pay her bill?

7. The weight of a tray of 36 eggs is 4.5 kg. What is the approximate weight of each egg?

8. The cost of a set of 14 football strips is £378. How much would just one strip cost?

9. Stanley fills a paddling pool with 18 buckets of water. This fills the paddling pool to its capacity of 288 litres. What is the capacity of the bucket?

10. The length of a roll of sticky tape is 10.37 m. A dispenser cuts pieces of 17 cm. How many pieces of sticky tape can be dispensed from each roll?

/10

Percentages

1. Write the following fractions as percentages.

   a) $\frac{1}{2}$ _____

   b) $\frac{1}{4}$ _____

   c) $\frac{3}{10}$ _____

   d) $\frac{3}{4}$ _____

2. Write the following decimals as percentages.

   a) 0.34 _____

   b) 0.57 _____

   c) 0.7 _____

   d) 0.03 _____

3. Write the following percentages as decimals.

   a) 49% _____

   b) 72% _____

   c) 5% _____

   d) 60% _____

4. What percentages of the grids below are shaded?

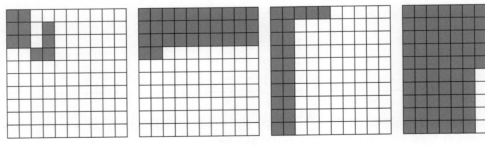

   a) _____%   b) _____%   c) _____%   d) _____%

Percentages

5. Calculate 50% of the following amounts.

   a) 42 kg _____ kg

   b) 64 litres _____ litres

   c) 3 km _____ km

   d) £70 £ _____

6. Calculate 30% of the following amounts.

   a) £120 £ _____

   b) 200 m _____ m

   c) £4.00 £ _____

   d) 600 kg _____ kg

7. There is a sale in a local game store. The sign says 25% off.

   Tim buys a game that originally cost £24.

   How much change does Tim get from £20?

   £ _____

8. Sarah puts £300 in a bank account. The money earns 7% interest per year.

   How much money does Sarah have in the account after one year's interest is added?

   £ _____

9. A man who weighs 92 kg decides to go on a diet. He loses 10% of his weight.

   What is his new weight?

   _____ kg

10. A road is 800 km long. The length is increased by 25%.

    How long is the road now?

    _____ km

/10

Ratio and proportion

1. What proportion of this square is shaded? Give your answer as a fraction.

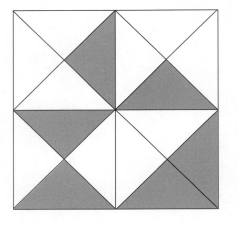

2. What proportion of this regular octagon is shaded? Give your answer as a fraction.

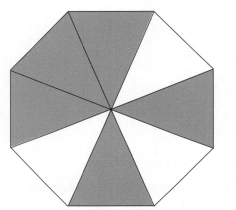

3. In a group of 10 children, four are boys and six are girls.
   What is the ratio of girls to boys?

   _____

4. There is a mixture of 14 red and yellow flowers in a bunch. The ratio of yellow to red is 6:1.
   What is the total number of yellow flowers in two bunches?

   _____

5. In a box of 40 marbles there are 24 black marbles and 16 white marbles.
   What is the ratio of black to white marbles?

   _____

Ratio and proportion

Look at the box of tiles shown.

6. What is the ratio of grey to white tiles?

_____

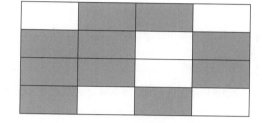

7. What proportion of the tiles are white?
Give your answer as a fraction.

8. In a group of 18 children, the ratio of boys to girls is 1:1.
How many boys and how many girls are there in the group?

Boys = _____

Girls = _____

9. Kelly has a birthday party. The ratio of children to adults is 4:1.
There are 24 children at the party. How many adults are there?

_____

10. Look at the cups of coffee on the tray.

What is the ratio of black to white cups?

_____

/10

Mixed 1

1. Write in words the value of the digit in bold in each number.

   a) 36**1** 028 _____

   b) 2 **5**27 815 _____

   c) **8** 100 325 _____

2. Estimate the answers to the questions below and then check your answers with a calculator.

Question	Estimate	Answer
6138 + 8432		
36 867 + 13 014		
4.97 + 18.01		
8211 − 7501		

3. Work out the value of y in the following equation.

   157 − y = 88 y = _____

4. Write in the missing fraction.

   $\frac{3}{9}$ + $\frac{1}{6}$ + ☐ = 1

5. Here are the weights of some children. Work out how much they weigh altogether.

   31.6 kg   27.38 kg   29.18 kg   31.07 kg   36.66 kg   27.5 kg

   _____ kg

Mixed 1

6. Add these numbers.

    a)   516 + 157 = _____

    b)   347 + 611 = _____

    c)   610 + 705 = _____

7. Richard went shopping and spent £12.60 on food, £5.50 on some socks and £10 on a scarf.
    How much money did he have left out of £30?

    £ _____

8. Calculate the answer to the multiplication below.

9. Work out the answer to the division below.

    21 | 1428

10. Andy puts £500 in a bank account. The money earns 8% interest per year.
    How much money does Andy have in the account after one year's interest is added?

    £ _____

    /10

Mixed 2

1. Order these decimals, starting with the **smallest**.

    a) 3.2   3.11   3.67   3.09   3.049

    b) 80.7   80.81   84.38   80.06   84.5

2. Estimate how much water is in this jug.

    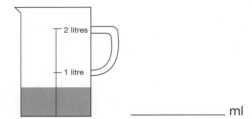

    _____ ml

3. $3b = 4a + c + 12$

    Find the value of b when $a = 7$ and $c = 2$.

    $b =$ _____

4. Write in the missing fraction.

    $\frac{1}{5} + \frac{1}{3} + \boxed{} = 1$

5. Convert the following quantities into decimal form.

    a) 7180 g   _____ kg

    b) 254 g   _____ kg

    c) 5888 ml   _____ litres

    d) 3469 cm   _____ m

6. Amy goes to the cinema and spends £5.40 on watching a film. She also buys a bag of sweets which costs £1.85.

    How much does Amy spend altogether?

    £ _____

Mixed 2

7. Take away 844 273 from 1 105 312.

8. Calculate the answer to the following multiplication.

$$
\begin{array}{r}
1914 \\
\times \quad 35 \\
\end{array}
$$

9. Work out the answer to the division below.

42 | 4788

10. A rope is 120 m long. The length is increased by 50% when another rope is tied to it. How long is the rope now?

_____ m

/10

Crossword fun

Try this maths crossword, using the clues below.

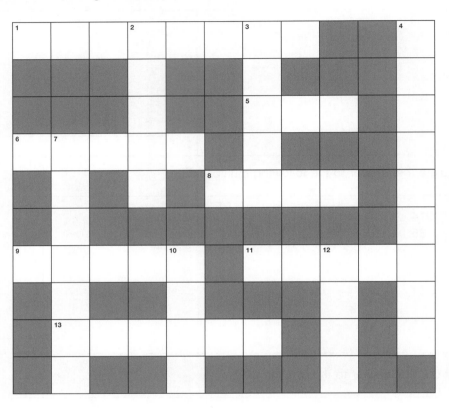

Across

1. Any three-sided polygon. (8)

5. The product of 5 and 2. (3)

6. $104 - 8^2$ (5)

8. Nothing at all. (4)

9. A square-based pyramid has five of these. (5)

11. Add all the numbers in a sum together to get this. (5)

13. The point of intersection of the x and y axis. (6)

Down

2. An angle of less than 90°. (5)

3. The metric version of a pint. (5)

4. Any polygon with sides of different lengths has this property. (9)

7. Any shape with eight sides. (7)

10. Another name for an operation in a calculation. (4)

12. The units for this could be seconds. (4)

Wordsearch fun

Can you find all the maths terms in this wordsearch?

D	E	I	M	P	R	O	P	E	R	F	R	A	C	T	I	O	N	B	E
D	E	G	A	F	S	R	R	Y	L	F	S	T	N	I	O	P	S	E	E
I	P	G	L	A	W	I	E	Q	U	A	L	V	B	C	F	A	D	O	T
V	L	Q	R	C	A	G	G	S	A	W	W	G	A	R	L	I	N	G	U
I	Q	F	B	E	S	I	E	Z	M	U	S	D	E	D	O	M	N	E	N
S	O	K	O	V	E	N	T	T	Q	R	M	Q	F	B	D	H	N	O	I
I	I	I	Z	D	V	C	N	A	O	R	E	P	U	A	R	P	O	M	M
O	Y	T	G	L	E	P	I	L	I	N	D	C	F	D	D	A	G	E	C
N	A	E	M	J	N	Y	I	L	C	O	I	P	A	R	O	R	Y	T	H
A	L	A	F	J	R	W	U	Y	U	I	A	T	D	I	E	G	L	R	L
K	I	L	O	M	E	T	R	E	C	X	N	R	Q	H	E	R	O	Y	W
C	T	A	C	T	Y	N	C	K	K	V	O	R	H	T	N	A	P	P	O
E	R	C	O	O	R	A	T	I	O	N	A	A	F	J	S	B	N	F	J
R	E	W	O	D	F	T	S	S	N	I	C	L	O	C	K	W	I	S	E
E	A	F	J	M	B	S	P	O	D	U	E	U	F	S	O	I	A	V	L
T	Z	X	V	I	P	P	G	S	T	N	Q	G	A	O	R	D	D	Z	C
R	L	A	A	H	L	A	I	A	G	P	U	E	S	R	A	T	I	A	R
A	P	E	E	I	N	W	S	T	I	N	U	R	D	E	Z	H	N	L	I
U	A	R	Y	O	D	R	H	S	F	F	S	D	W	Z	T	S	P	W	C
Q	E	A	N	E	G	A	T	I	V	E	T	A	I	H	E	I	G	H	T

Area	Geometry	Origin
Bar graph	Height	Polygon
Compass	Improper fraction	Point
Circle	Integer	Quarter
Clockwise	Kilometre	Ratio
Cuboid	Kite	Regular
Division	Litre	Sphere
Degree	Length	Sum
Edge	Median	Tally
Equal	Minute	Third
Even	Negative	Unit
Face	Nonagon	Width
		Zero

2-D shapes

1. Fill in the gaps to make the following sentences correct.

   A three-sided polygon is a _____ .

   An eight-sided polygon is an _____ .

   A five-sided polygon is a _____ .

   A seven-sided polygon is a _____ .

   A ten-sided polygon is a _____ .

2. An equilateral triangle has a perimeter of 45 cm. What is the length of each side?

   _____ cm

3. Look at the following shapes and match each of them to the correct description.

   has no lines of symmetry

   not a polygon

   interior angles add to make 180°

   is a quadrilateral

   is a pentagon

4. On the grid below, complete the drawing to make an irregular quadrilateral.

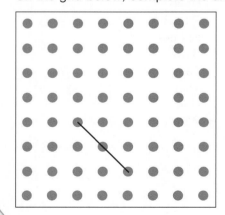

5. The radius of a circle is 54 cm. What is the diameter of the circle?

Diameter = _____

6. Put a tick in the shapes which have any parallel sides.

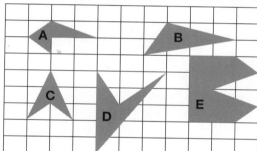

7. Here are five shapes. Tick the two which have lines of symmetry.

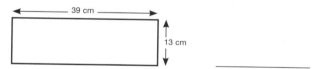

8. How many squares that each have a perimeter of 26 cm will fit into the rectangle below?

39 cm

13 cm

_____

9. Look at this circle inside a square. What is the radius of the circle if the square has a perimeter of 32 cm?

Radius = _____ cm

10. Angle c = 90° and angle b = 60°, so what is angle a?

a = _____°

/10

3-D shapes

1. How many **faces** do the following 3-D shapes have?

   a) Cube _____ face(s)

   b) Cylinder _____ face(s)

   c) Sphere _____ face(s)

2. How many **edges** do the following 3-D shapes have?

   a) Cuboid _____ edge(s)

   b) Cone _____ edge(s)

   c) Square-based pyramid _____ edge(s)

3. How many **vertices** do the following 3-D shapes have?

   a) Cylinder _____ vertices

   b) Cube _____ vertices

   c) Triangular-based pyramid _____ vertices

4. Which two of the following are correct nets for a cube?

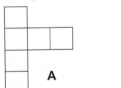

A

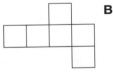

B

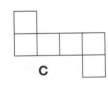

C

D

_____ and _____

5. What is the volume of a cube with an edge that measures 7 cm?

   _____ cm^3

3-D shapes

6. What is the surface area of this cuboid?

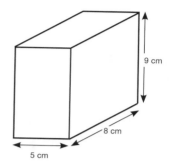

9 cm

8 cm

5 cm

_____ cm²

7. What is the volume of this open-top tank?

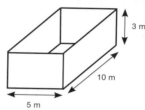

3 m

10 m

5 m

_____ m³

8. A cube has a volume of 1000 cm³. What is the area of each face?

_____ cm²

9. What is the volume of the cube which has this net?

6 cm

_____ cm³

10. Which of the following are correct nets for a cuboid?

A

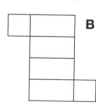

B

C

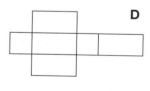

D

_____ and _____

/10

Geometry and angles 1

1. Using a ruler, complete the diagram below to make a symmetrical shape.

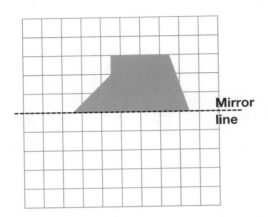

Mirror line

2. Using a ruler, draw the reflection of this shape.

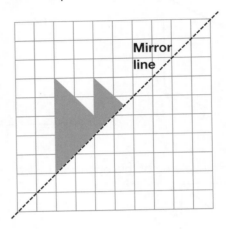

Mirror line

3. Look at the shapes below and put a tick inside the shapes with at least one line of symmetry.

 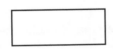 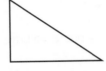

4. Which of these letters are symmetrical?

F H B J _____ and _____

5. Look at the shape in the diagram below left. Write the letter of the shape that would be its reflection.

Letter _____

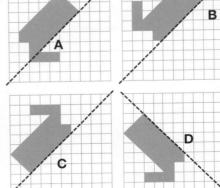

Geometry and angles 1

6. Join the angles to the correct labels.

reflex angle
acute angle
right angle
obtuse angle

7. Estimate the size of the acute angles below. Do not use a protractor.

$x =$ _____ °

$y =$ _____ °

8. Estimate the size of the obtuse angles below. Do not use a protractor.

$a =$ _____ °

$b =$ _____ °

9. Look at the parallelogram below and calculate the angle x. Do not use a protractor.

$x =$ _____ °

70°

x

10. Calculate angle x in this isosceles triangle. Do not use a protractor.

$x =$ _____ °

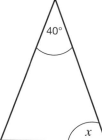

40°

x

/10

Geometry and angles 2

1. Measure angle x accurately. Use a protractor.

$x =$ _____ °

2. Measure angle z accurately. Use a protractor.

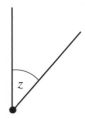

$z =$ _____ °

3. Measure all the angles in this triangle. Use a protractor.

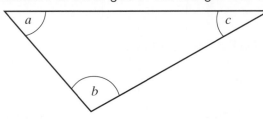

$a =$ _____ °

$b =$ _____ °

$c =$ _____ °

4. Measure angle y accurately. Use a protractor.

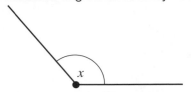

$y =$ _____ °

5. Measure accurately the two angles below. Use a protractor.

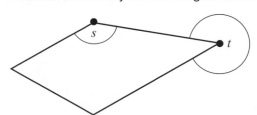

$s =$ _____ °

$t =$ _____ °

6. Calculate the angle x in the triangle below.

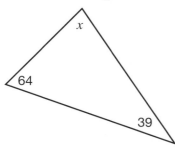

$x = $ _____ °

7. Look at the following regular polygon. What is the internal angle z?

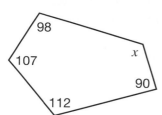

$z = $ _____ °

8. Calculate the angle x in the pentagon below.

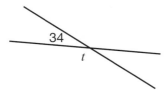

$x = $ _____ °

9. Calculate the angle t.

$t = $ _____ °

10. Calculate the angle z.

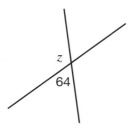

$z = $ _____ °

/10

Coordinates

1. Plot these coordinates on the grid below.

J (1 , 7)   K (6 , 5)
L (9 , 13)   M (4 , 10)

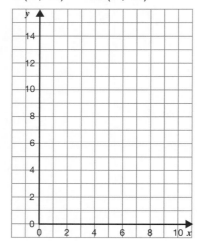

2.

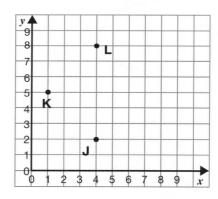

a) Where is the park? (,   )

b) Where is the market? (,   )

c) Where is the pool? (,   )

3. Write down the coordinates M, N, O and P.

M = (,   )   N = (,   )
O = (,   )   P = (,   )

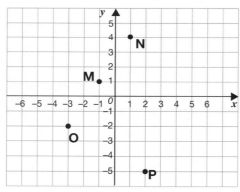

4. Plot point M on the grid below to complete the square JKLM.

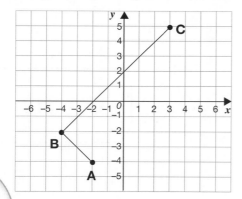

5. Plot point D on the grid below and complete the rectangle ABCD.

Coordinates

6. Which quadrants are the letters A, B, C and D in?

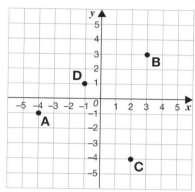

A = Quadrant _____

B = Quadrant _____

C = Quadrant _____

D = Quadrant _____

7. Draw the triangle below reflected in the x axis.

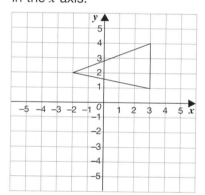

8. Plot the points A, B, C and D on the graph below.

A (4 , –3)   B (–1 , 2)
C (–4 , –1)   D (1 , 2)

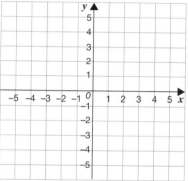

9. Plot the points A, B, C, D, E, and F then join them together to make the capital letter E.

A (2 , 2)   B (–2 , 2)
C (–2 , –1)   D (2 , –1)
E (–2 , –4)   F (2 , –4)

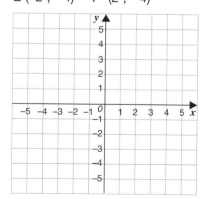

10. Translate the shape below so that Point A is at (1 , 2).

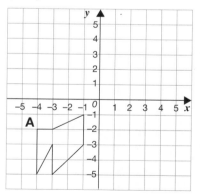

/10

Reading scales and converting units

1. Convert these units of length.

   a) 3 m = _____ cm

   b) 45 mm = _____ cm

   c) 3.5 km = _____ m

   d) 4 miles = _____ km

2. Convert these units of weight.

   a) 3500 g = _____ kg

   b) 750 kg = _____ tonnes

   c) 4.06 kg = _____ g

   d) 4.2 tonnes = _____ kg

3. Convert these units of capacity.

   a) 3.5 cl = _____ ml

   b) 3450 ml = _____ litres

   c) 9.052 litres = _____ ml

   d) 457 ml = _____ cl

4. What is the reading on the scale below?

   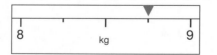

   _____ kg

5. How much water is in this jug?

   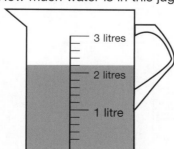

   _____ litres

Reading scales and converting units

6. Measure the lengths of these three lines with a ruler.

a) 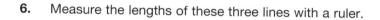 _____

b)  _____

c)  _____

7. How much more flour do you need to add to these kitchen scales to make 1.9 kg?

_____

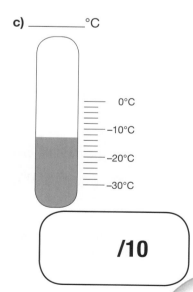

8. When opened, a tap lets 100 ml of water through every second.
How much water passes through the open tap in 2.5 minutes? _____ ml

9. A man walks 1.4 km to work every day and at the end of the day walks back home again.
How many kilometres does the man walk in a normal five-day working week?

_____ km

How many miles is this equivalent to? _____ miles

10. Write down the readings on these three thermometers.

a) _____°C

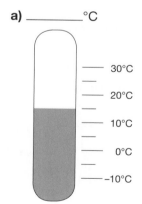

b) _____°C

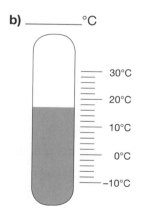

c) _____°C

/10

1. What fraction of 3 hours is 30 minutes?

$$\frac{\boxed{}}{\boxed{}}$$

2. How many seconds are there in 45 minutes?

_____ seconds

3. Jon sets off from school at 3:30 p.m. He then goes to see his Grandma and eventually gets home at 19:45.

How many minutes after Jon left school did he arrive at home?

_____ minutes

4. How many minutes are there in 24 hours?

_____ minutes

5. Here is a calendar for the month of September in a particular year.

September						
Sun	Mon	Tue	Wed	Thu	Fri	Sat
			1	2	3	4
5	6	7	8	9	10	11
12	13	14	15	16	17	18
19	20	21	22	23	24	25
26	27	28	29	30		

a) School starts on the second Wednesday of the month. What date is that?

_____

b) Jack arrives back from holiday on the last Friday in August. What date is that?

_____

6. a) Billy gets to the cinema at 17:30. The film starts at 18:25.

How long must Billy wait before the film starts?

_____ minutes

b) The film lasts for 115 minutes. What time does it finish? Give your answer in 24-hour clock time.

_____

7. Here is a calendar for the month of July in a particular year.

July						
Sun	Mon	Tue	Wed	Thu	Fri	Sat
				1	2	3
4	5	6	7	8	9	10
11	12	13	14	15	16	17
18	19	20	21	22	23	24
25	26	27	28	29	30	31

Sally goes on holiday for 10 days, and she arrives back on the 4th of July.
What day of the week did Sally leave on?

_____

8. What is $\frac{2}{3}$ of 2 hours? _____

9. Sasha can run a kilometre in 4 minutes and 15 seconds.
If Sasha always runs at the same speed, how long will it take her to run 7 kilometres?

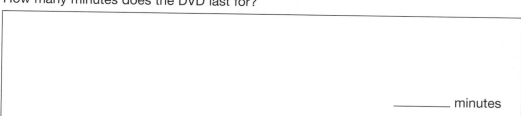

10. James puts on a DVD at twenty-five past five. The DVD finishes at quarter to eight.
How many minutes does the DVD last for?

_____ minutes

/10

Perimeter, area and volume

1. What is the perimeter of the shape below?

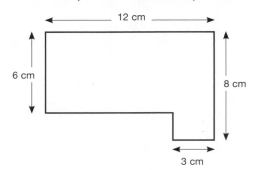

12 cm

6 cm

8 cm

3 cm

_____ cm

2. Look at this shape on the centimetre square grid.

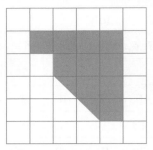

What is the area of this shape?

_____ cm²

3. A regular pentagon has a perimeter of 32 cm.

What is the length of each side of the pentagon? _____ cm

4. Estimate the area of the shape below.

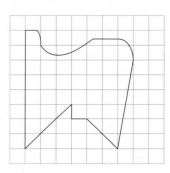

Area = _____ squares

5. Look at this shape on a centimetre square grid.

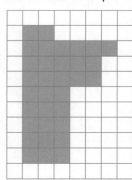

What is the perimeter of this shape?

_____ cm

Perimeter, area and volume

6. Look at the cube below and calculate its volume and surface area.

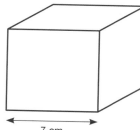

Volume = _____ cm³

Area = _____ cm²

7 cm

7. Tick the two shapes below which have the same area.

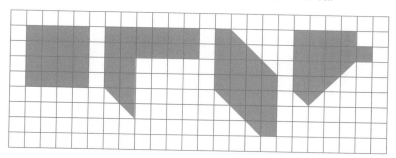

8. Tick the two shapes below which have the same perimeter.

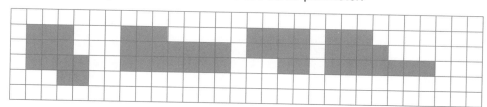

9. Calculate the area of this parallelogram.

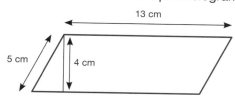

13 cm

5 cm   4 cm

Area = _____ cm²

10. What is the area of the isosceles

triangle here? _____ cm²

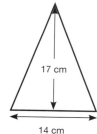

17 cm

14 cm

/10

Tables, charts and graphs 1

The bar graph below shows the amount of money a shop took in one week.

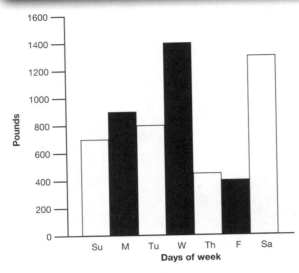

1. How much money did the shop take at the weekend?

£ _____

2. How much money did the shop take on Monday?

£ _____

The bar line graph below shows how far some children can jump.

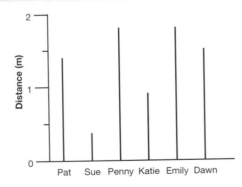

3. How far can Emily jump? _____ m

4. How much further can Pat jump than Katie? _____ m

Tables, charts and graphs 1

The line graph shows the accumulative rainfall during March in one year.

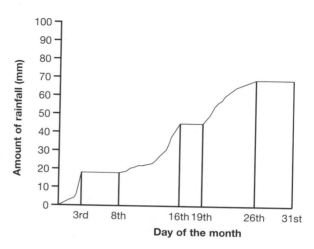

5. How much rainfall was there in the whole month? _____ mm

6. How much rainfall was there between the 16th and 31st of the month? _____ mm

7. Why does the graph flatten off in three places?

_____

8. True or false? There were 21 wet days during the month. _____

There are 300 ice lollipops of four different types in a freezer. The number of each type is represented by the chart.

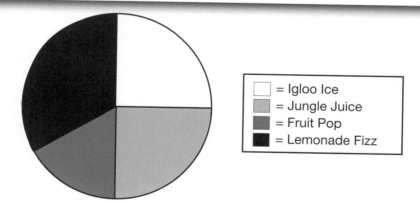

☐ = Igloo Ice
▨ = Jungle Juice
▨ = Fruit Pop
■ = Lemonade Fizz

9. How many Jungle Juice lollipops are there? _____

10. Approximately how many Fruit Pop lollipops are there? _____

/10

Tables, charts and graphs 2

The number of chocolate bars sold at a school tuck shop is shown below.

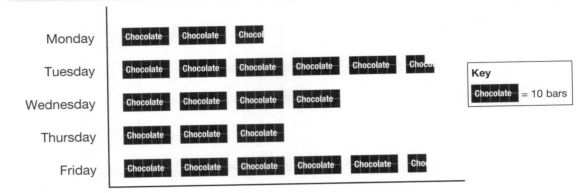

1. How many chocolate bars were sold on Monday?

    _____ bars

2. How many more chocolate bars were sold on Friday than on Wednesday?

    _____ bars

Look at the bar chart showing pocket money received by six children.

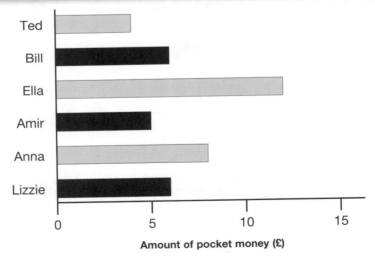

3. How much pocket money did Bill get?   £ _____

4. How much money did the children receive altogether?   £ _____

Tables, charts and graphs 2

The pie chart below shows the type of pets 100 children have.

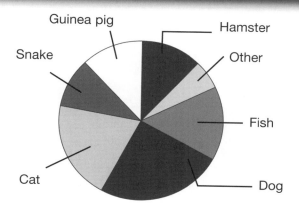

5. Approximately how many children have a dog or a cat? _____

6. Estimate the number of children who have a pet snake. _____

7. Estimate how many more children have a dog than a hamster. _____

The temperature in a conservatory was measured regularly and recorded on the graph.

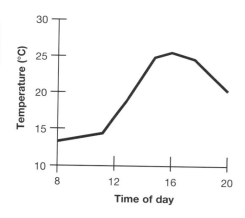

8. At what time was the last temperature reading taken? _____

9. What was the approximate temperature at 4 p.m.? _____ °C

10. When did the temperature first reach 20°C? _____

/10

Mixed 3

1. Draw all the diagonals on the octagon below.

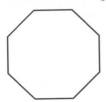

2. What is the volume of this cuboid?

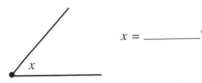

5 cm

8 cm

2 cm

Volume = _____ cm³

3. Use a ruler and draw the reflection of this shape.

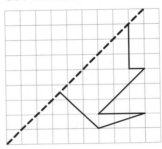

4. Measure angle x accurately. Use a protractor.

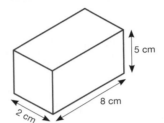

$x =$ _____ °

x

5. Write down the coordinates of A, B, C and D.

A = (,   )   B = (,   )   C = (,   )   D = (,   )

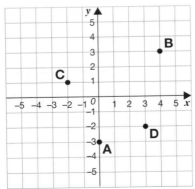

6. Calculate the mean in this list of 10 numbers.

8, 7, 7, 9, 4, 12, 10, 7, 11, 9 _____

7. Measure the lengths of these three lines with a ruler.

a) 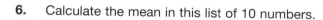 _____ cm

b) _____ _____ cm

c) _____ _____ cm

8. What fraction of 2 hours is 15 minutes?

9. A group of children do a sponsored walk. Here is the amount of money each child raised:

Name	Amount (£)
Jess	10.20
Kate	12.90
Paul	8.50
Wendy	14.00
Raul	13.40

What is the mean amount of money raised per child? £_____

10. What is the area of this right-angled triangle?

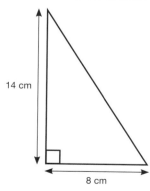

14 cm

8 cm

Area = _____ cm²

/10

1. Angle $a = 40°$ and angle $b = 141°$. What is angle c?

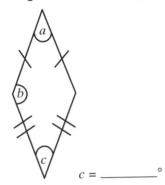

$c =$ _____ °

2. What is the volume of a cube with this net?

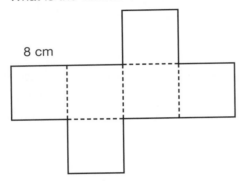

8 cm

Volume = _____ cm³

3. Estimate the size of the angles below. Do not use a protractor.

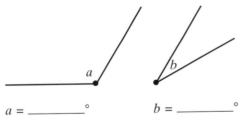

a b

$a =$ _____ ° $b =$ _____ °

4. Calculate the angle x in the triangle below.

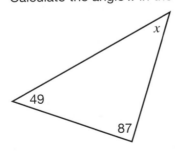

x

49

87

$x =$ _____ °

5. Plot the points D, E, F and G on the graph below.

D (–2 , –4)   E (3 , –2)   F (0 , 3)   G (–2 , 2)

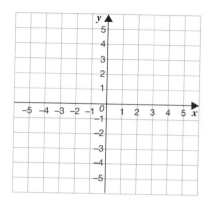

6. Find the mean of this set of 10 numbers.

15, 12, 8, 15, 8, 10, 10, 17, 13, 20 _____

7. What is the reading on the scale below?

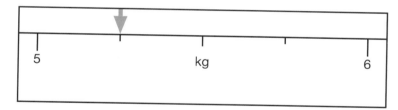

_____ kg

8. Micky sets off for work at 7:30 a.m. He arrives at work at 8:55 a.m. How many minutes after Micky left home did he arrive at work?

_____ minutes

9. Find the mean of this set of numbers.

3, 8, 4, 3, 2, 4, 7, 6, 9, 5, 4 _____

10. Calculate the area of this parallelogram.

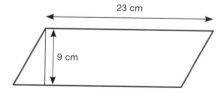

Area = _____ cm²

/10

Sudoku fun

Each of these puzzles will take about 10 minutes!

Sudoku is a logic puzzle. It is presented as a square grid with 9 squares to a side. Thick grid lines emphasise each block of 9 squares. The grid is partially filled with the numbers 1 through to 9. To solve the puzzle, the empty squares are filled in so that each row, column and block contains each of the numbers 1 through to 9. There is only one correct answer.

29.

	8			2	7		3	1
		7	9	1	4		6	
1				3	8			5
7	6	8	2	4	1		9	3
			3	5	6	7		
4	3	5	8		9	2	1	6
6		3	4		2	1		
	7	2	1		5		4	
5							2	8

30.

5		2	7			9	3	
1				2			7	
	7	9		3	1	6	8	2
6	8	5	1			7	2	
			9		7			
	9	3			2	1	4	6
9	2	1	3	7		4	6	
	5			9				3
	4	6			5	8		7

31.

9		6	1	4	8		3	
			2				6	1
	8	2	3	6		4		
4	2		5	7		1		3
8				3				5
3		5		8	2		7	4
			5	4	3	2		
2	7				9			
	3		6	2	1	9		7

32.

3		5		8	7		1	
2		6				4	7	
	1		2	4			8	6
8		2		9		3		
	6	4	3		2	8	9	
	3		6			7		2
4	3	1		5	9		2	
	2	8				9		7
	9		8	2	6			4

Fun with squares

How many squares can you find on the picture below? Look carefully, there are more than you think!

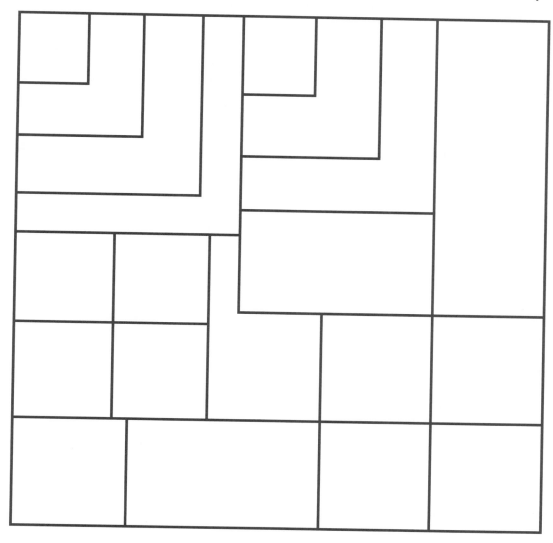

_____ squares

Progress report

Record how many questions you got right and the date you completed each test.
This will help you to monitor your progress.

Test 1 /10 Date _____	**Test 2** /10 Date _____	**Test 3** /10 Date _____	**Test 4** /10 Date _____	**Test 5** /10 Date _____
Test 6 /10 Date _____	**Test 7** /10 Date _____	**Test 8** /10 Date _____	**Test 9** /10 Date _____	**Test 10** /10 Date _____
Test 11 /10 Date _____	**Test 12** /10 Date _____	**Test 13** /10 Date _____	**Test 14** /10 Date _____	**Test 15** If you got all of the clues in less than 10 minutes, score yourself 10 marks. Date _____
Test 16 If you got all of the clues in less than 10 minutes, score yourself 10 marks. Date _____	**Test 17** /10 Date _____	**Test 18** /10 Date _____	**Test 19** /10 Date _____	**Test 20** /10 Date _____
Test 21 /10 Date _____	**Test 22** /10 Date _____	**Test 23** /10 Date _____	**Test 24** /10 Date _____	**Test 25** /10 Date _____
Test 26 /10 Date _____	**Test 27** /10 Date _____	**Test 28** /10 Date _____	**Test 29** If you complete the puzzle in less than 10 minutes, score yourself 10 marks. Date _____	**Test 30** If you complete the puzzle in less than 10 minutes, score yourself 10 marks. Date _____
Test 31 If you complete the puzzle in less than 10 minutes, score yourself 10 marks. Date _____	**Test 32** If you complete the puzzle in less than 10 minutes, score yourself 10 marks. Date _____	**Test 33** If you found the right number of squares in less than 10 minutes, score yourself 10 marks. Date _____		

Answers: Maths 10-Minute Tests, age 10-11

Test 1
1. 10 835
2. **a)** two hundred **b)** two thousand **c)** twenty thousand
3. **a)** 1553 **b)** 4224 **c)** 3530
4. **a)** 1067, 2799, 2809, 2851, 4001
   b) 6001, 6099, 6430, 6515, 7000
5. **a)** 1 031 710, 103 826, 87 271, 17 001, 12 483
   b) 4 280 338, 2 984 988, 583 200, 560 200, 100 999
6. **a)** 4.03, 4.09, 4.099, 4.2, 4.27
   b) 20.01, 20.72, 20.9, 24.27, 24.4
7. $\frac{7}{2}, \frac{12}{5}, \frac{7}{3}, \frac{3}{2}, \frac{10}{9}$
8. **a)** Billy **b)** Eric **c)** Jon
9. **a)** B **b)** A **c)** D
10. **a)** Grant **b)** Smith

Test 2
1. **a)** 440, 370, 900, 250
   b) 6480, 7050, 8890, 5810
   c) 29 840, 18 000, 21 000, 99 510
2. **a)** 200, 1000, 700, 300
   b) 5800, 4200, 6700, 3400
   c) 23 100, 57 900, 31 000, 90 000
   d) 128 300, 451 200, 927 000, 370 000
3. **a)** 1000, 3000, 6000, 8000
   b) 12 000, 30 000, 68 000, 37 000
   c) 222 000, 709 000, 502 000, 199 000
4. Child 1 = 1.2 m, Child 2 = 1.3 m, Child 3 = 1.2 m
   Child 4 = 1.4 m, Child 5 = 1.3 m, Child 6 = 1.5 m

5.
Question	Estimate (between these numbers)	Answer
2129 + 3454	5300 to 5700	5583
24 783 + 15 031	39 000 to 40 000	39 814
7.92 + 15.01	22 to 23	22.93
5203 − 3487	1500 to 2000	1716

6. Answers between 2100 ml and 2400 ml
7. Answers between 12 kg and 14 kg
8. Answers between 180 cm and 190 cm
9. Answers between 60 minutes and 62.5 minutes
10. Answers between 2500 weeks and 2600 weeks

Test 3
1.
3	6	12	24	**48**	**96**

2.
160	80	40	20	**10**	**5**

3.
□	○	△	□	□	○	△	□

4.
−14	−8	**−2**	4	10	16

Test 4
1. 67
2. 216
3. 40
4. Blue marbles = 25
   Yellow marbles = 75
5. Adults = 50   Children = 150
6. **a)** 4, 8, 12, 16, 20, 24, 28, 32, 36
   b) 28 and 1, 14 and 2, 7 and 4
7. Shortest = 9 cm   Longest = 18 cm
8. 4 years old
9. 18
10. 42

Test 5
1. 8.2
2. **a)** five hundredths
   b) five tenths
   c) five thousandths
3. **a)** 0.6 **b)** 2.8 **c)** 7.64 **d)** 0.18
4. **a)** 3.6 **b)** 20.4 **c)** 42.7 **d)** 26.04
5. **a)** 1.6 **b)** 11.2 **c)** 13.89 **d)** 37.83
6.
	Old amount	New amount
Carrots	1200 g	2.4 kg
Potatoes	2.5 kg	5 kg
Tomatoes	0.45 kg	0.9 kg
Onions	3	6
Peas	300 g	0.6 kg

7. £71.56
8. 163.63 kg
9. 220 litres
10. 170 m

Test 6
1. **a)** 71 **b)** 109 **c)** 143
2. **a)** 436 **b)** 729 **c)** 1235
3. **a)** 106 **b)** 122 **c)** 101
4. **a)** 10 352 **b)** 47 101 **c)** 107 891
5. 251 815
6. £7.35
7. £79.39
8. 155 m
9. £17.02
10. 829 + 164 = 993

Test 7
1. **a)** 46 **b)** 58 **c)** 33
2. **a)** 213 **b)** 239 **c)** 146
3. **a)** 48 **b)** 16 **c)** 42
4. **a)** 715 **b)** 68 556 **c)** 607 569
5. 797 788
6. £7.73
7. £3.60

5.
13	5	**−3**	−11	−19	**−27**

6. 8°C
7. 8°C
8. −5°C
9. 6°C
10. 24 hours

8. 3.3 kg
9. 8 minutes
10. 944 − 398 = 546

Test 8
1. $4\frac{2}{7}$
2. $\frac{5}{8}$
3. $1\frac{5}{12}$
4. $3\frac{7}{10}$
5. $\frac{1}{2}$
6. **a)** $\frac{1}{6}$ **b)** $\frac{1}{8}$ **c)** $\frac{1}{16}$
7. $\frac{3}{2}$ $\frac{13}{6}$ $\frac{29}{8}$ $\frac{19}{5}$ $\frac{12}{3}$
8. $\frac{4}{15}$ or $\frac{8}{30}$
9. $\frac{7}{24}$
10. $3\frac{1}{2}$ or $3\frac{6}{12}$ or $\frac{42}{12}$

Test 9
1. **a)** 27.1, 271, 2710 **b)** 30.9, 309, 3090 **c)** 460, 4600, 46000
2. 40 066
3. 105 915
4. 361 974
5. £20 784
6. £601.64
7. 45 kg or 45 000 g
8. £282.91
9. 16.383 l or 16 383 ml
10. 28.635 m

Test 10
1. **a)** 2.4, 0.24, 0.024 **b)** 35.7, 3.57, 0.357 **c)** 259.8, 25.98, 2.598
2. 82
3. 37
4. 83
5. 148
6. £27
7. 0.125 kg or 125 g
8. £27
9. 16 litres
10. 61

Test 11
1. **a)** 50% **b)** 25% **c)** 30% **d)** 75%
2. **a)** 34% **b)** 57% **c)** 70% **d)** 3%
3. **a)** 0.49 **b)** 0.72 **c)** 0.05 **d)** 0.6
4. **a)** 10% **b)** 32% **c)** 23% **d)** 65%
5. **a)** 21 kg **b)** 32 litres **c)** 1.5 km **d)** £35
6. **a)** £36 **b)** 60 m **c)** £1.20 **d)** 180 kg
7. £2
8. £321
9. 82.8 kg
10. 1000 km

Test 12
1. $\frac{6}{16}$ or $\frac{3}{8}$
2. $\frac{5}{8}$
3. 6:4 or 3:2
4. 24
5. 24:16 or 12:8 or 6:4 or 3:2
6. 10:6 or 5:3
7. $\frac{6}{16}$ or $\frac{3}{8}$

8. Boys = 9, Girls = 9
9. 6
10. 7:5

Test 13

1. **a)** one thousand **b)** five hundred thousand **c)** eight million

2.

Question	Estimate	Answer
6138 + 8432	**14 500**	14 570
36 867 + 13 014	**50 000**	49 881
4.97 + 18.01	**23**	22.98
8211 − 7501	**700**	710

3. 69
4. $\frac{1}{2}$
5. 183.39 kg
6. **a)** 673 **b)** 958 **c)** 1315
7. £1.90
8. 89 889
9. 68
10. £540

Test 14

1. **a)** 3.049, 3.09, 3.11, 3.2, 3.67
   b) 80.06, 80.7, 80.81, 84.38, 84.5
2. Answers between 600 ml and 720 ml
3. 14
4. $\frac{7}{15}$
5. **a)** 7.18 kg **b)** 0.254 kg
   c) 5.888 litres **d)** 34.69 m
6. £7.25
7. 261 039
8. 66 990
9. 114
10. 180 m

Test 15

T	R	I	A	N	G	L	E			I
		C			I					R
		U			T	E	N			R
F	O	R	T	Y		R				E
	C	E		Z	E	R	O			G
	T					I				U
F	A	C	E	S		T	O	T	A	L
	G			I				I		A
	O	R	I	G	I	N		M		R
	N			N				E		

Test 16

D		I	M	P	R	O	P	E	R	F	R	A	C	T	I	O	N	
D	E		F		R	R				T	N	I	O	P				E
I		G	A		I	E	Q	U	A	L				D				T
V		R	C	G	G								I			G	U	
I		E		I	E		M	U	S			O				E	N	
S	K		E	N	T	T		M			B		H	N	O	I		
I	I	D	V	N	A		E	U			P	O	M	M				
O	T	G	E		I	L		D	C		D		A	G	E			
N	E		N			L		I		R	R	Y	T					
	L					Y		A		I		G	L	R				
K	I	L	O	M	E	T	R	E		N		H	R	O	Y			
T							R	T	A	P								
R	C		R	A	T	I	O		A		B							
R	E	O				N		C	L	O	C	K	W	I	S	E		
E		M	S	O		E	U			I		I		L				
T		P	G		N	G	O	D		C								
R	A	H	A		G		E	R	T		R							
A	E	E	N	S	T	I	N	U	R	E	H		I					
U	R	O		H	S				Z			C						
Q	E	A	N	E	G	A	T	I	V	E		H	E	I	G	H	T	

Test 17

1. A three-sided polygon is a *triangle*.
   An eight-sided polygon is an *octagon*.
   A five-sided polygon is a *pentagon*.
   A seven-sided polygon is a *heptagon*.
   A ten-sided polygon is a *decagon*.
2. 15 cm
3.

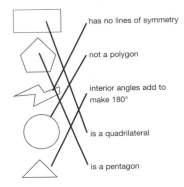

has no lines of symmetry

not a polygon

interior angles add to make 180°

is a quadrilateral

is a pentagon

4. Any four-sided shape with at least one side a different length.
5. 108 cm or 1.08 m
6.

7.

8. 12
9. 4 cm
10. 105°

Test 18

1. **a)** 6 **b)** 3 **c)** 1
2. **a)** 12 **b)** 1 **c)** 8
3. **a)** 0 **b)** 8 **c)** 4
4. B and C
5. 343 cm³
6. 314 cm²
7. 150 m³
8. 100 cm²
9. 216 cm³
10. B and D

Test 19

1.

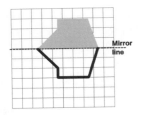

2.

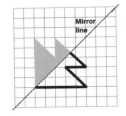

3.

4. H and B
5. C
6.

reflex angle

acute angle

right angle

obtuse angle

7. Answers in between the following:
   $x = 20°$ to $30°$ and $y = 65°$ to $75°$
8. Answers in between the following:
   $a = 130°$ to $140°$ and $b = 95°$ to $105°$
9. 110°
10. 70°

Test 20

1. 130° (126° to 134° is acceptable)
2. 40° (36° to 44° is acceptable)
3. $a = 50°$ $b = 100°$ $c = 30°$
   (Answers ± 3°)
4. 235° (Answers ± 4°)
5. $s = 140°$ $t = 320°$
   (Answers ± 4°)
6. 77°
7. 120°
8. 133°
9. 146°
10. 116°

Test 21

1.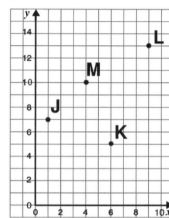
2. **a)** Park (17, 12) **b)** Market (3, 13)
   c) Pool (16, 1)
3. M = (−1, 1) N = (1, 4) O = (−3, −2)
   P = (2, −5)
4.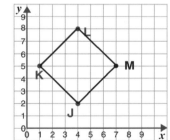
5.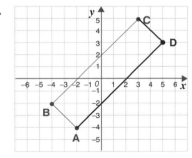
6. A = III, B = I, C = IV, D = II

7.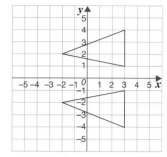

8.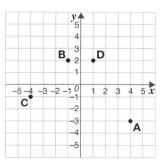

9.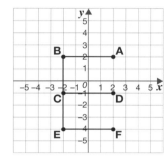

10.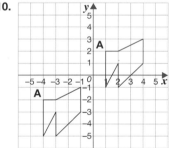

Test 22

1. **a)** 300 cm **b)** 4.5 cm **c)** 3500 m
   d) 6.45 km
2. **a)** 3.5 kg **b)** 0.75 tonnes **c)** 4060 g
   d) 4200 kg
3. **a)** 35 ml **b)** 3.45 litres **c)** 9052 ml
   d) 45.7 cl
4. 8.75 kg or 8 kg 750 g
5. 2.2 litres or 2 litres and 200 ml
6. **a)** 7.6 cm or 76 mm **b)** 4.2 cm or
   42 mm **c)** 5.5 cm or 55 mm
7. 1.1 kg or 1 kg 100 g or 1100 g
8. 15 000 ml
9. 14 km, 8.68 miles
10. **a)** 15°C **b)** 17°C **c)** −13°C

Test 23

1. $\frac{1}{6}$
2. 2700 seconds
3. 255 minutes
4. 1440 minutes
5. **a)** 8th September
   b) 27th August
6. **a)** 55 minutes
   b) 20:20
7. Thursday
8. 80 minutes or 1 hour and 20
   minutes
9. 29 minutes and 45 seconds
10. 140 minutes

Test 24

1. 40 cm
2. 11 cm²
3. 6.4 cm
4. 35-39 squares
5. 30 cm
6. Volume 343 cm³, Area 294 cm²
7.
8.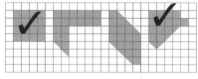
9. 52 cm²
10. 119 cm²

Test 25

1. £2000
2. £900
3. 1.8 m
4. 0.5 m
5. 69 mm (accept 68 to 70)
6. 24 mm (accept 22 to 27)
7. It did not rain on those days.
8. false
9. 75
10. 50 (accept 45 to 55)

Test 26

1. 26
2. 14
3. £6
4. £41 (accept 40 to 42)
5. 45 (accept 42 to 48)
6. 10 (accept 7 to 13)
7. 13 (accept 10 to 15)
8. 20:00 or 8 p.m.
9. 26°C (accept 25°C to 27°C)
10. Answers between 12:45 and 13:45
    (12:45 p.m. and 1:45 p.m.)

Test 27

1.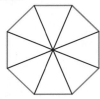

2. 80 cm³

3.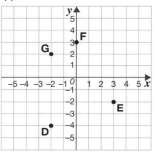

4. 50°
5. A = (0 , –3) B = (4, 3) C = (–2, 1)
   D = (3, –2)
6. 8.4
7. **a)** 4.3 cm **b)** 2.8 cm **c)** 5.1 cm
8. $\frac{1}{8}$
9. £11.80
10. 56 cm²

Test 28

1. 38°
2. 512 cm³
3. Accept a = 115°–125°, and b = 25°–35°
4. 44°
5.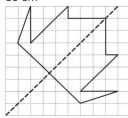

6. 12.8
7. 5.25 kg
8. 85 minutes
9. 5
10. 207 cm²

Test 29

9	8	6	5	2	7	4	3	1
3	5	7	9	1	4	8	6	2
1	2	4	6	3	8	9	7	5
7	6	8	2	4	1	5	9	3
2	1	9	3	5	6	7	8	4
4	3	5	8	7	9	2	1	6
6	9	3	4	8	2	1	5	7
8	7	2	1	6	5	3	4	9
5	4	1	7	9	3	6	2	8

Test 30

5	6	2	7	8	4	9	3	1
1	3	8	6	2	9	5	7	4
4	7	9	5	3	1	6	8	2
6	8	5	1	4	3	7	2	9
2	1	4	9	6	7	3	5	8
7	9	3	8	5	2	1	4	6
9	2	1	3	7	8	4	6	5
8	5	7	4	9	6	2	1	3
3	4	6	2	1	5	8	9	7

Test 31

9	5	6	1	4	8	7	3	2
7	4	3	2	9	5	8	6	1
1	8	2	3	6	7	4	5	9
4	2	9	5	7	6	1	8	3
8	6	7	4	1	3	2	9	5
3	1	5	9	8	2	6	7	4
6	9	1	7	5	4	3	2	8
2	7	4	8	3	9	5	1	6
5	3	8	6	2	1	9	4	7

Test 32

3	4	5	6	8	7	2	1	9
2	8	6	9	1	5	4	7	3
7	1	9	2	4	3	5	8	6
8	7	2	5	9	4	3	6	1
1	6	4	3	7	2	8	9	5
9	5	3	1	6	8	7	4	2
4	3	1	7	5	9	6	2	8
6	2	8	4	3	1	9	5	7
5	9	7	8	2	6	1	3	4

Test 33
21 squares

KS2 Success

Age 10-11

English

10-Minute Tests

Nick Barber

Sample page

clear instructional text

topic being covered

test number for quick reference

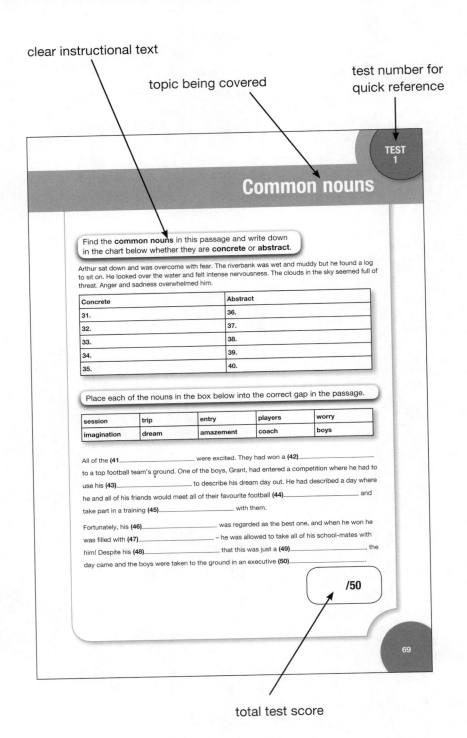

TEST 1

Common nouns

Find the **common nouns** in this passage and write down in the chart below whether they are **concrete** or **abstract**.

Arthur sat down and was overcome with fear. The riverbank was wet and muddy but he found a log to sit on. He looked over the water and felt intense nervousness. The clouds in the sky seemed full of threat. Anger and sadness overwhelmed him.

Concrete	Abstract
31.	36.
32.	37.
33.	38.
34.	39.
35.	40.

Place each of the nouns in the box below into the correct gap in the passage.

session	trip	entry	players	worry
imagination	dream	amazement	coach	boys

All of the (41)_____ were excited. They had won a (42)_____ to a top football team's ground. One of the boys, Grant, had entered a competition where he had to use his (43)_____ to describe his dream day out. He had described a day where he and all of his friends would meet all of their favourite football (44)_____ and take part in a training (45)_____ with them.

Fortunately, his (46)_____ was regarded as the best one, and when he won he was filled with (47)_____ – he was allowed to take all of his school-mates with him! Despite his (48)_____ that this was just a (49)_____, the day came and the boys were taken to the ground in an executive (50)_____.

/50

69

total test score

66

Contents

Common nouns

Underline the **common nouns** in these sentences.
There may be more than one in a sentence.

1. The boy sat down.

2. Every girl wore make-up.

3. None of the bands were any good.

4. The river burst its banks and flooded the town.

5. Tara scrubbed her feet.

6. Rain fell on Tom's umbrella.

7. The puppy bit the chair.

8. Canoes are used to travel on rivers.

9. The desk collapsed when Fred sat on it.

10. All the answers from the class were the same.

11. Cars and trains were used by the girls.

12. The hat did not fit.

13. Soldiers marched past the monument.

14. Lisa's goldfish was orange.

15. Every boy ate his sandwiches.

Circle the **common abstract** nouns in these sentences.
There may be more than one in a sentence.

Example: (Joy) filled their faces.

16. The day ended.

17. Robbie was filled with happiness.

18. The girls showed great intelligence when they did the test.

19. The football supporters were suffering from extreme boredom.

20. Bravery is a good quality to have.

21. The woman's kindness affected everybody greatly.

22. There was no love lost between the boxers.

23. It took great courage for Denise to jump out of the aeroplane.

24. Wilf felt great joy when he scored.

25. "Your imagination will cause you fear," said Dawn.

26. Beauty is only skin deep.

27. Revenge was not necessary for the boxer.

28. Please help people suffering with loneliness.

29. The workers were rewarded for their loyalty.

30. The juggler demonstrated great skill.

Common nouns

> Find the **common nouns** in this passage and write down in the chart below whether they are **concrete** or **abstract**.

Arthur sat down and was overcome with fear. The riverbank was wet and muddy but he found a log to sit on. He looked over the water and felt intense nervousness. The clouds in the sky seemed full of threat. Anger and sadness overwhelmed him.

Concrete	Abstract
31.	36.
32.	37.
33.	38.
34.	39.
35.	40.

> Place each of the nouns in the box below into the correct gap in the passage.

session	trip	entry	players	worry
imagination	dream	amazement	coach	boys

All of the **(41)**_____ were excited. They had won a **(42)**_____

to a top football team's ground. One of the boys, Grant, had entered a competition where he had to

use his **(43)**_____ to describe his dream day out. He had described a day where

he and all of his friends would meet all of their favourite football **(44)**_____ and

take part in a training **(45)**_____ with them.

Fortunately, his **(46)**_____ was regarded as the best one, and when he won he

was filled with **(47)**_____ – he was allowed to take all of his school-mates with

him! Despite his **(48)**_____ that this was just a **(49)**_____, the

day came and the boys were taken to the ground in an executive **(50)**_____.

/50

Pronouns

In each of these sentences, change the underlined word or words to the correct pronoun.

1. **Robert** married Tara.   _____

2. Robert married **Tara**.   _____

3. **My sister and I** went shopping.   _____

4. Michelle brought **her present**.   _____

5. **Emma** has got a twin sister.   _____

6. **The goldfish** was swimming.   _____

7. **Laura** had long hair.   _____

8. Josh spoke to **the boys**.   _____

9. Ali joined **the others**.   _____

10. **The singers** hired Joe as their manager.   _____

Read this passage and circle the correct pronouns from the choices given.

Zak the pop star wanted his assistant, Lucy, to get **(11) him/her/them** a new microphone for his act. The last microphone he had used wasn't very good because **(12) he/she/it** had broken within five minutes of the start of his concert. **(13) She/He/They** had warned Zak that buying cheap microphones was not a good idea because of this very problem. Lucy was rather fed up with telling **(14) him/her/them** about such things and, in fact, she was considering getting a new job. **(15) She/He/They** had worked together since the early part of Zak's career, but now **(16) she/he/they** felt that it was time to move on and get a fresh start. Zak wasn't aware of Lucy's feelings and still treated **(17) her/him/them** as though there were no problems. **(18) She/He/They** went and bought a new microphone and tested **(19) it/him/her** before she handed it over to **(20) him/her/them**.

Pronouns

In each of these sentences, tick the correct pronoun for the underlined words.

21. The professor never gives **the students** homework.

   a) me ☐   **b)** them ☐   **c)** you ☐

22. I gave the book to **my little niece**.

   a) her ☐   **b)** us ☐   **c)** him ☐

23. The boys are playing with **their console games**.

   a) it ☐   **b)** them ☐   **c)** her ☐

24. My mother is sending a gift to **Robbie**.

   a) me ☐   **b)** her ☐   **c)** him ☐

25. I guessed **the answer**.

   a) she ☐   **b)** her ☐   **c)** it ☐

26. Mia is going to see **Becky**.

   a) her ☐   **b)** him ☐   **c)** me ☐

27. Shut **the door**, please.

   a) it ☐   **b)** them ☐   **c)** us ☐

28. Can you tell **the people** the way to Port Vale's ground?

   a) you ☐   **b)** them ☐   **c)** us ☐

29. The gifts are for **Claire**.

   a) him ☐   **b)** her ☐   **c)** you ☐

30. Can you give directions to **my wife and me**?

   a) her ☐   **b)** me ☐   **c)** us ☐

/30

In each sentence, circle the verb which makes the most sense.

Example: Stuart **played/ate/chose** his bass guitar very well.

Answer: Stuart **played** his bass guitar very well.

1. Paul **ran/scoffed/ate** all the way to the shops to get there before they closed.

2. Riaz didn't **realise/fry/torment** how much money he'd made.

3. **Eating/Squinting/Locating** jelly was not an option because of her special diet.

4. Jessica started to **tweak/shake/scribble** with fear.

5. The referee **disguised/digested/spoiled** the game for the fans.

6. Barney did not **cough/speak/loan** to his friends all night.

7. "Don't **dribble/squeak/eat** peas with a spoon!" said Ellie.

8. Lucie **frowned/gargled/smiled** with happiness.

9. The light **exploded/lit/smothered** when the fuse box broke.

10. Joanne **smoked/waited/shouted** loudly across the room.

Choose an appropriate verb to complete each sentence. There are lots of possible answers.

11. Chris _____ the drums.

12. Craig _____ off his chair.

13. Nick _____ presents for his nieces.

14. Irene _____ until dinner time and then woke up.

15. Deepa _____ away because she didn't like having her photograph taken.

16. Dave's camera had been _____ from his car.

17. Peter's kitchen was _____ to make it look as good as new.

18. Sylvia _____ what time it was because she'd lost her watch.

19. Arthur _____ a new part for the broken clock all by himself.

20. Aysha's painting _____ in the exhibition.

Verbs

Look at the words in the table. Tick to show whether each one is a verb, a noun, both or neither. The first one is done for you.

Word	Just a verb	Just a noun	Both	Neither
talking			✔	
21. silliness				
22. run				
23. joke				
24. cry				
25. document				
26. fear				
27. show				
28. tablet				
29. sympathy				
30. happy				
31. question				
32. talk				
33. decommission				
34. pretty				
35. clever				
36. blissful				
37. smell				
38. awkwardly				
39. study				
40. dump				

/40

Verb-subject agreement

In these sentences, circle the correct form of the verb so that each one makes sense.

1. Donna **was running/were running** the event.

2. Meena and Tracy **was organising/were organising** the reception.

3. Brenton **is coming/are coming** to the match.

4. Sean and David **is going/are going** to the cinema.

5. Mike and Neil **are/is** neighbours.

6. Scientists **are working/is working** on a cure for the common cold.

7. Noise **was/were** a problem for people living next to the main road.

8. The results **is/are** final.

9. Why did the others ask if they **was/were** coming along?

10. Marie **is getting/are getting** ready for the meal.

Tick whether these sentences have the correct form of verb and subject agreement. The first one is done for you as an example.

Sentence	Correct verb-subject agreement	Incorrect verb-subject agreement
The boys **are** playing football tonight.	✔	
11. Madison and her friends is going out.		
12. Emma is changing her job.		
13. Nobody knew what Elijah were doing.		
14. Tara and Mark are going to Leeds.		
15. The supermarket were opening a new branch.		
16. What was they thinking of?		
17. Hannah weren't happy.		
18. Kathryn and Tom were cleaning.		
19. Nobody knew that Helena were a secret agent!		
20. James was getting ready.		

Verb-subject agreement

Complete these sentences with the correct
form of the verb, using **is**, **are**, **was** or **were**.

Example: Marie _____ working last week but not next week.

Answer: Marie **was** working last week but not next week.

21. James _____ going to see Angus next week.

22. Michelle and Emma _____ staying at their mum's house when the power
cut happened.

23. Andrew _____ taking pictures of the holiday when he dropped his camera.

24. Courtney _____ finishing her essay when the teacher said that the exam
time was up.

25. Rodney _____ going on holiday soon.

26. Kurt _____ living in Kentucky, at this moment in time.

27. Nobody knew if Dorothy _____ telling the truth about her lottery win.

28. Johanna _____ baking gingerbread men for tonight's meal.

29. Ed _____ looking for his keys yesterday.

30. Richard and Bruce _____ getting ready to perform at this very moment.

Write five sentences, making sure you use **is**, **are**, **was** or **were** in
each of them. There are lots of different answers that you might give,
but use each of the four words at least once.

31. _____

32. _____

33. _____

34. _____

35. _____

/35

Past tense and present perfect

Change these sentences into the past tense by changing each highlighted word for a past tense single word verb.

1. Mia **eats** broccoli. _____

2. Eleanna **performs** in amateur dramatics. _____

3. Alan **stands** outside the school gates. _____

4. Samantha **rides** her horse. _____

5. Alexandra **has** long hair. _____

6. Kellie **giggles**. _____

7. Robbie **sings** to himself, quietly. _____

8. Mark **invents** things. _____

9. Alicia **sits** in silence. _____

10. Tom **knits** socks for babies. _____

Complete this table, using the different forms of the past tense. An example has been done for you.

Verb	Present perfect tense	Simple past tense
arrive	I have arrived	I arrived
11. find		
12. study		
13. teach		
14. do		
15. call		
16. shout		
17. catch		
18. clap		
19. bring		
20. go		

Past tense and present perfect

Change these sentences from their current tense into the past tense, **changing as few words as possible**. Write down the words you change.

Example: Marie is eating fish and chewing vegetables at the same time.

Answer: Marie **was** eating fish and chewing vegetables at the same time.

21. The boys are losing at half time.   _____

22. Chuck sings and plays guitar in a band.   _____

23. Catherine buys strange clothes.   _____

24. Liam wears fancy dress costumes at parties.   _____

25. Laura rarely asks questions.   _____

26. Isaac smiles a lot, especially when he concentrates. _____

27. Whitney's loud voice fills the room.   _____

28. Ari walks into the classroom when she is ready.   _____

29. Samuel invests in Internet-based companies.   _____

30. Maisie enjoys school holidays because she can lie in. _____

Make the present perfect tense from these sets of prompt words.

Example: Prompt words - I / study / German

Answer: I have studied German

31. He / eat / jambalaya   _____

32. They / go / Wales   _____

33. They / read / that magazine   _____

34. He / live / here for ten months   _____

35. You / know / Michelle / for ten years _____

36. We / be / there for two weeks   _____

37. I / find / my key   _____

38. He / drink / too much tea   _____

39. They / catch / the bus   _____

40. She / go / to Stoke   _____

/40

The passive voice

Change each of these sentences into the passive voice.

1. Did the police officer catch the thief? _____

2. Did your mum pick you up? _____

3. He doesn't open the book. _____

4. He opens the door. _____

5. I draw a picture. _____

6. She pays a lot of money. _____

7. They don't help you. _____

8. They wear blue shoes. _____

9. We set the table. _____

10. You did not write the letter. _____

Using these key words, write sentences in the simple present tense, passive voice.

Example: Prompt words - the book / write

Answer: The book is written.

11. the book / not / read _____

12. the car / wash _____

13. the documents / print _____

14. the food / not / eat _____

15. the letter / send _____

16. the litter / throw away _____

The passive voice

17. the shoes / buy _____

18. the shop / not / close _____

19. the songs / not / sing _____

20. the window / open _____

21. the race / run _____

22. the work / do _____

23. the process / activate _____

24. the dance / perform _____

25. the play / act _____

Re-write these sentences in the simple past tense, passive voice.

26. A thief stole my car. _____

27. Did he send the letter? _____

28. Did you tell them? _____

29. I did not tell them. _____

30. She didn't win the prize. _____

31. She sang a song. _____

32. Somebody hit me. _____

33. They didn't let him go. _____

34. They didn't make their beds. _____

35. We stopped the bus. _____

/35

Adjectives

Circle the adjectives in these sentences.

1. The dull, dreary day carried on as it had started.

2. Happy people work hard.

3. Exciting football matches happen frequently.

4. The cute hamsters ate their food.

5. Henry walked past the tall, imposing gate.

6. Faye's jewellery was expensive.

7. Loud shouts were heard from the playground.

8. The skilful forward raced past the defender.

Place adjectives in the following sentences. There are lots of possible answers.

9. The _____ girl sang very well.

10. After the _____ party, everyone had to tidy up.

11. Before the _____ meeting, Don sorted out his notes.

12. Before the meeting, Don had to sort out his _____ notes.

13. Every game was as _____ as the first one.

14. Petra's _____ uncle bought her presents for her birthday.

15. Ellie disliked eating _____ cabbage.

Place adjectives in this passage to make it sound mysterious and spooky. There are lots of possible answers, but all of the adjectives you choose should help to build up the right kind of mood.

The **(16)** _____ man walked through the **(17)** _____ gate

and saw the **(18)** _____ house. He walked through the

(19) _____ garden and approached the **(20)** _____

door. The house looked **(21)** _____ and **(22)** _____, but

he knocked on the door anyway. After a few **(23)** _____ moments the door

opened and a **(24)** _____ figure stood in front of him. The man walked into the

(25) _____ hallway.

Adjectives

Now complete the passage again, but this time choose adjectives that will make it sound light-hearted and jolly.

The **(26)** _____ man walked through the **(27)** _____

gate and saw the **(28)** _____ house. He walked through the

(29) _____ garden and approached the **(30)** _____ door.

The house looked **(31)** _____ and **(32)** _____, but he

knocked on the door anyway. After a few **(33)** _____ moments the door

opened and a **(34)** _____ figure stood in front of him. The man walked into the

(35) _____ hallway.

In these sentences there is an adjective in brackets. Change it into the comparative form.

36. A boulder is (heavy) _____ than a feather.

37. Our car is (fast) _____ than yours.

In these sentences there is an adjective in brackets. Change it into the superlative form.

38. It was the (big) _____ shock in the tournament.

39. Owen was the (noisy) _____ person in the class.

40. January is the (bad) _____ month of the year.

/40

Verbs fun

Below is a list of verbs – find them in the grid. They may be found backwards, forwards, up, down or diagonally in any direction.

RUN	CREATE	FINISH
TALK	KICK	FLY
WANDER	WHISTLE	FLAP
SCORE	CHEER	TRAP
RACE	TACKLE	ENCOURAGE
WIN	LOSE	CROSS
INJURE	BEAT	

A	C	K	E	N	C	O	U	R	A	G	E	F	X	E	P	K	P	Q	C
P	H	R	Q	G	T	G	C	H	K	F	X	I	E	G	N	X	T	B	V
V	L	U	M	S	U	D	I	O	D	N	H	N	Q	M	E	T	L	T	L
N	J	K	R	X	L	T	V	W	C	K	J	I	U	W	W	X	T	M	V
U	T	O	R	P	W	S	N	Q	H	R	J	S	A	V	U	X	R	E	B
M	F	J	O	A	A	R	W	K	W	N	E	H	F	G	O	K	S	O	I
B	Z	G	B	W	C	B	B	A	F	H	S	A	I	R	Y	K	O	E	C
I	D	Y	P	P	H	E	T	K	N	A	I	N	T	U	N	V	X	H	I
U	E	B	U	M	Z	M	W	Y	C	Z	M	S	W	E	I	I	P	R	S
R	U	N	V	J	I	J	I	I	F	I	T	I	T	K	L	A	T	S	B
K	F	B	W	M	W	P	N	V	D	N	K	G	H	L	N	L	O	R	W
U	V	U	V	D	G	M	X	N	L	G	A	H	F	B	E	R	L	P	V
S	F	I	N	D	W	D	E	E	D	D	T	L	L	G	C	O	W	U	G
R	L	C	Q	M	R	R	Y	A	P	Y	L	K	T	W	X	R	Y	F	K
E	A	H	W	U	O	R	A	O	A	T	A	E	B	A	C	X	A	S	J
D	F	E	H	C	E	I	J	Y	R	S	P	P	K	T	Q	X	J	F	J
N	L	E	S	P	U	W	B	X	T	D	B	A	Y	O	P	W	G	J	Y
A	Y	R	O	F	J	O	F	G	U	Y	G	N	L	R	I	E	T	N	P
W	T	A	C	K	L	E	K	D	E	S	O	L	E	F	I	H	S	F	G
P	T	I	N	J	U	R	E	G	X	W	S	P	M	L	B	J	A	K	Q

Adjectives fun

Complete the crossword below by using the clues. All of the answers are adjectives.

Across

2. Twitchy and a bit scared
4. Huge
7. Not noisy
13. In a good mood
14. Not wanting to do something
16. Unusual, often in a good way
18. Not hot
19. Pretty, or attractive
20. Frightened

Down

1. In a bad mood
3. Not rough
5. Dull and overcast
6. Not dull
8. Hard to believe; amazing
9. Not very nice
10. Almost too small to be seen
11. Unable to be achieved
12. Not soft
15. Intelligent
17. Hurt

Adverbs

In these sentences there is an adjective in brackets. Change it into an adverb, so that the sentence will make sense.

1.   The athlete ran _____ (quick) to the finish line.

2.   Robbie _____ (amazing) released 50 songs on his new album.

3.   Tara smiled _____ (reluctant) when she saw that she had to eat the carrots.

4.   Dev ambled _____ (lazy) to the shed.

5.   _____ (Astonishing), Jennifer had done her homework.

6.   _____ (Lucky), Danny had put the chicken in the oven on time.

7.   Kristina had _____ (fortunate) won the lottery.

8.   Peter had _____ (clever) found a way to solve the puzzle.

9.   The snow in June had _____ (crazy) forced the cricket match to be cancelled.

10. Katrina walked _____ (cautious) to the shops.

Not all words that end in **ly** are adverbs. Read these sentences and tick whether the word ending in "**ly**" is an adverb or an adjective.

Sentence	Adverb	Adjective
11. The **holy** man spoke well.		
12. Ray **nervously** ate the food.		
13. **Ugly** creatures are scary.		
14. **Smelly** streets need cleaning.		
15. **Carefully**, Sam packed her bags.		
16. Caesar **triumphantly** entered Rome.		
17. The teacher's **kindly** ways made him popular.		
18. Emma disliked walking in the **chilly** weather.		
19. Fred's **surly** looks scared people off.		
20. Rita walked rather **anxiously** into the exam room.		

Adverbs

Place an appropriate adverb in each of these sentences – there could be several possible answers but try to use a different adverb each time.

21. _____, Becky answered the first question.

22. Tom _____ wrote his answers down.

23. Clair tidied up the kitchen _____.

24. Peter took out the bags _____.

25. _____, Ramona strode into the room.

26. The nurse _____ attended to her duties.

27. Tom _____ ate his dinner.

28. Despite the bad weather, the boys managed the walk _____.

29. The river ran _____ through the deep gorge.

30. Rick _____ put on his shoes.

31. _____, Natasha ate her ice-cream.

32. Lisa performed _____ in the test.

33. Without asking, Jagram _____ ate the sweets.

34. In order to win the race, Gemma ran _____.

35. The wind whistled _____ around the house.

36. The ballerina stepped _____ across the stage.

37. The horses _____ entered the field.

38. Danny missed a chance when he shot _____ at the goalkeeper.

39. Dean _____ made excuses for his naughty behaviour.

40. Bill waited _____ for the trouble to calm down.

/40

Modal verbs and adverbs

1. We **might/could/will** go to the cinema.

2. We **may/will/could** take part in the sponsored run.

3. They **shall/might/may** win the lottery.

4. They **did/might/may** go swimming.

5. We **could/should/will** stick to our resolutions.

Change the underlined adjective to an adverb in these sentences.

6. She was a <u>happy</u> girl.

   She played _____.

7. The singer had a <u>beautiful</u> voice.

   She sang _____.

8. He was always <u>honest</u>.

   He spoke with her _____.

9. The sun was very <u>strong</u>.

   It was shining _____.

10. We felt <u>sad</u> at the leaving party.

    We looked at each other _____.

11. He was an <u>expert</u> guitarist.

    He played it _____.

12. They were very <u>enthusiastic</u> about applauding.

    They applauded _____.

13. You are very <u>energetic</u>.

    You dance _____.

Modal verbs and adverbs

14. He was a <u>dangerous</u> rider.

He rode _____.

15. Grandfather was a <u>frequent</u> visitor.

He visited _____.

> Add adverbs into the spaces in this passage.

Mary walked **(16)** _____ towards the shop. It was

(17) _____ shut, but that didn't stop Mary. She knocked

(18) _____ on the door and shouted **(19)** _____ at the

upstairs window. A window **(20)** _____ opened and a head

(21) _____ peered out.

"Who's that?" said a voice, **(22)** _____.

"It's one of your customers!" replied Mary **(23)** _____. "It's past your opening

time. Why aren't you open?"

There was no reply, but the window was **(24)** _____ shut and there were

sounds of movement going on, before a figure appeared at the shop door. There was the sound

of shuffling keys and the lock **(25)** _____ turned and the door opened.

"I'm sorry – my alarm didn't go off. Please come in." Mary shrugged her shoulders

(26) _____ and strode **(27)** _____ into the shop.

"What would you like?" asked the shop assistant **(28)** _____.

"Have you got any chocolate biscuits?" said Mary, while fiddling **(29)** _____ in

her bag for her purse.

"I'm sorry," replied the assistant **(30)** _____ - "We're a chemist's...."

/30

Adverbials

In these sentences there is an adjective in brackets. Change it into an adverb, in order for the sentence to make sense.

Example: The runner ran the race (quick).

Answer: The runner ran the race **quickly**.

1. The singer sang the song (beautiful)_____.

2. Dan complained (bitter) _____ about the referee's decision.

3. Lily smiled (coy) _____.

4. Roberto took the photograph (clever) _____.

5. (Incredible) _____ their first song went straight to number 1.

6. Rosie (speedy) _____ completed her work.

7. Joe smiled (awkward) _____ when the teacher praised him.

8. The rain poured (heavy) _____ over the town.

9. Dan jumped (nervous) _____ when he heard the loud music.

10. Ed strolled (lazy) _____ into the classroom.

Not all words that end in "**ly**" are adverbs. Read these sentences and decide whether the word ending in "**ly**" is an adverb or an adjective.

Sentence	Adverb	Adjective
11. The girl smiled **happily**.		
12. Ellie **ravenously** devoured her dinner.		
13. **Smelly** cheese is the best.		
14. **Chilly** winds blew through everywhere.		
15. **Delicately**, they tiptoed into the house.		
16. The athlete **speedily** raced to the line.		
17. The **ugly** insects frightened them.		
18. The explorer **courageously** walked for miles.		
19. Emily wore the dress **beautifully**.		
20. Rohan's **kindly** manner won him friends.		

Adverbials

Underline the adverbial of manner in these two sentences.

21. The boys were playing merrily.

22. She was running as fast as possible.

Underline the adverbial of place in these two sentences.

23. We saw her there.

24. He searched everywhere he could.

Underline the adverbials of time in these four sentences.

25. They start work at lunchtime.

26. They usually go to school in a car.

27. She went to their house yesterday.

28. I saw that film last week.

Underline the adverbials of probability in these two sentences.

29. Perhaps the weather will be cold.

30. He is definitely coming to the concert.

Underline all five adverbs in this passage.

31–35. He yawned sleepily and then suddenly realised it was time for work. Immediately he leapt out of bed and hurriedly threw his clothes on. Falling clumsily down the stairs, he cracked his knee against the wall.

/35

Homophones

Underline the correct option in bold in each sentence.

1. No one could **accept/except** the referee's decision.

2. Everyone **accept/except** the referee knew what was going on.

3. The children were not **aloud/allowed** to go shopping.

4. The children were heard to complain **aloud/allowed** when they could not go shopping.

5. "Sack the **bored/board**!" cried the annoyed fans.

6. "I'm **board/bored**," said the annoyed fan.

7. The prisoner was out on **bale/bail**.

8. "How much does a **bale/bail** of hay weigh?" he asked the farmer.

9. "Don't **brake/break** that vase!" shouted Alice.

10. "Don't use the **break/brake** like that on the motorway!" cried the instructor.

11. The politicians decided to **canvas/canvass** opinion.

12. The artist used a **canvas/canvass** for his portrait.

13. "**Check/Cheque** your oil," said the mechanic.

14. "Can I pay by **check/cheque**?" asked the bank customer.

15. Her shoes **complemented/complimented** her hat, as they were the same colour.

16. Noel **complemented/complimented** his sister on her choice of hat and dress.

17. The **council/counsel** was in charge of organising the waste disposal services.

18. The **council/counsel** gave advice in the courtroom.

19. Tammy had a sweet **desert/dessert** after her meal.

20. Jonathan had driven all the way across the **desert/dessert** for his meal.

21. There was a cold **draught/draft** in the room.

22. Lesley had done the first **draft/draught** of her essay.

23. The two men fought a **dual/duel**.

24. The two men had **duel/dual** responsibility.

25. The ill boy **feinted/fainted** and had to have medical help.

Homophones

26. The swordsman **feinted/fainted** and tricked his opponent into a false move.

27. The Queen **formerly/formally** announced the opening of Parliament.

28. The Prime Minister had **formerly/formally** been the Home Secretary.

29. "**Hear/Here** I am!"

30. "Can you **hear/here** me?"

31. The lazy worker was described as **idle/idol** by his boss.

32. The building had a carving of a religious **idle/idol** outside.

33. The caterpillar produced the **larva/lava**.

34. The volcano produced the **larva/lava**.

35. The shopping bags were as heavy as **lead/led**.

36. The supporters were **led/lead** to the ground by a policeman on a motorbike.

37. The skyscraper was struck by **lightening/lightning**.

38. The pale colours had a **lightning/lightening** effect on the room.

39. Nobody wanted to **lose/loose** the cup final.

40. The football manager pulled his tie **lose/loose** as the game went into extra time.

41. No one **knew/new** what the result might be.

42. The **knew/new** members of the team helped us to win.

43. Jenny didn't like filling in **personal/personnel** information on the form.

44. The **personal/personnel** department dealt with recruitment.

45. Fiona didn't like travelling on a **plane/plain**.

46. The open country was very **plane/plain**.

47. The hunters chased their **pray/prey**.

48. The vicar asked the congregation to **pray/prey**.

49. "Keep **quiet/quite**!" whispered the guide.

50. "That's **quite/quiet** enough, thank you," muttered the teacher.

/50

Silent letter words

In each of the sentences below, there is a word with a silent letter missing. Underline the word and rewrite it with its missing letter.

1. The builder hit his thum with the hammer. _____

2. No one douted that the answer was correct. _____

3. The forward feined injury to get a penalty. _____

4. The girl's legs were covered with nat bites. _____

5. Nobody new what was up with the new boy. _____

6. Thomas did not get a receit for the presents he bought. _____

7. Robert had a seudonym on the Internet message board, to hide his identity. _____

8. It was cold, so Catherine rapped up warm. _____

9. The angry dog nashed its teeth. _____

10. The famous film star rote in Jemma's autograph book. _____

In the passage below are 10 words with a silent **b** in them. Underline the 10 words.

11–20. Barry broke the table when an earthquake that felt like a bomb went off. He climbed back into his chair and combed his hair, which had been messed up in the explosion. A few crumbs from his dinner floated in the air and landed on his knee. His face and both his upper limbs were numb with shock, but he kept calm. He wondered whether the plumbing in the house had been affected. Without doubt, he was indebted to the strong table for protecting him from the quake, although his thumb had been trapped and squashed by it.

Silent letter words

Here are 10 words that contain a silent **k** and their meanings. Match the words with their meanings.

21. knight   a tied coil of thread or perhaps rope

22. knave   bang on something

23. knit   be aware of

24. knee   an item used to cut things

25. knot   a word implying that someone is of low class or a troublemaker

26. know   the mid-way joint on the leg

27. knock   a finger joint

28. knowledge   someone who might have worn armour, who has the title "Sir"

29. knife   awareness

30. knuckle   to create material from thread, often with needles

Write **correct** or **incorrect** to say which of the following words are spelled correctly.

31. matress – something you lie on   _____

32. attitude – an opinion or feeling towards something   _____

33. narled – twisted and old looking   _____

34. foreigner – a person not from where you live   _____

35. neumonia – a disease   _____

36. sychiatrist – a person who tries to understand the workings of a person's mind   _____

37. wrinkle – a bendy line, often in skin   _____

38. pseudonym – a made up name   _____

39. plumer – a person who fixes baths, taps and pipes   _____

40. psychic – a person who can see into the future and/or read minds   _____

/40

Synonyms and antonyms

Synonyms are words that have similar meanings. Write a synonym for each of these words.

1. picture _____
2. lamp _____
3. conceal _____
4. snooze _____
5. lane _____
6. bravery _____
7. cold _____
8. large _____
9. hot _____
10. eat _____
11. build _____
12. hurry _____
13. push _____
14. buy _____
15. look _____
16. car _____
17. field _____
18. grumble _____
19. cloak _____
20. journey _____

Underline the appropriate word in the brackets to complete each sentence.

21. Pramila [crushed cracked] the egg into the cake mixture.

22. Dad found a [box crate] of matches and lit the candles on the cake.

23. The librarian [arranged planned] the books neatly on the shelf.

24. It was hot so Mark asked for a glass of [cold frosty] water.

25. We [soar fly] out to Greece on Thursday.

26. The joke was so funny, we laughed till we [mourned cried].

27. I [brushed swept] my hair before I went out.

28. Mum bought a [pipe tube] of stripy toothpaste.

29. Uncle Martin will [collect gather] us from school later.

30. I chose a [shiny glittery] red apple.

Synonyms and antonyms

An antonym is a word that has the opposite meaning to that of another word. Write antonyms for these words.

31. expensive _____

32. wide _____

33. find _____

34. dead _____

35. increase _____

36. tiny _____

37. buy _____

38. tall _____

39. break _____

40. open _____

Use a suitable prefix to make antonyms for these words.

41. _____ + grateful = _____

42. _____ + obedient = _____

43. _____ + correct = _____

44. _____ + proper = _____

45. _____ + healthy = _____

46. _____ + logical = _____

47. _____ + possible = _____

48. _____ + realistic = _____

49. _____ + order = _____

50. _____ + polite = _____

/50

tious/cious and tial/cial spellings

Choose the correct spelling in each case.

1. The student was very **ambitious/ambicious** because he wanted to get a top degree.

2. The jewels were very **pretious/precious**.

3. The tiger was very **ferotious/ferocious**.

4. The girl was very **consciencious/conscientious** in her work.

5. The boy made a **facecious/facetious** comment which upset him.

6. The story was not true – it was **fictitious/ficticious**.

7. His spelling was **atrocious/atrotious**.

8. Fred's laughter was **infecious/infectious**.

9. The fruit was regarded as very **nutricious/nutritious**.

10. The answer was completely **fallatious/fallacious**.

11. They were very **cautious/caucious** entering the spooky cave.

12. The critic's ideas were a bit **pretencious/pretentious**.

13. The boxer was **semi-conscious/semi-contious** after the fight.

14. The child musician was very **precocious/precotious**.

15. He had a **voratious/voracious** appetite for curry.

Complete these sentences by putting tious or cious correctly on the endings of the words.

16. The cruel man was very mali_____.

17. The film star was very gra_____ in her gifts to charity.

18. The disease was very infec_____.

19. The boxer's attitude was very pugna_____.

20. The wise man was exceedingly saga_____ with his advice.

tious/cious and tial/cial spellings

21. The story was completely ficti_____.

22. The result was quite conten_____ because it was so close.

23. The meal was scrump_____.

24. He was awake and fully cons_____.

25. The children's behaviour proved to be very vexa.

Choose the correct spelling in each case.

26. Wearing strong boots in the mud was **essential/essencial**.

27. Wearing water-proofs was **crutial/crucial** if they weren't going to get soaked.

28. She used a **fatial/facial** scrub to get clean.

29. Playing loud music at 1.30am was regarded as **anti-sotial/anti-social**.

30. The i**nitial/inicial** reactions to the film were quite good.

31. They had won a **potencial/potential** jackpot of millions.

32. They were given **preferencial/preferential** treatment at the restaurant because they knew the owner.

33. The man was an expert at **marcial/martial** arts.

34. The athlete had good **spacial/spatial** awareness.

35. The large meal was quite **substantial/substancial** for them.

36. The students had on-site **residencial/residential** accommodation.

37. John and Imran only had **parcial/partial** success in completing the course.

38. The rain was **torrencial/torrential**.

39. Doing the revision was **benefitial/beneficial**.

40. Their fantastic hotel was almost **palacial/palatial**.

/40

ant/ent and ancy/ency spellings

Choose the correct spelling in each case.

1. He had a good job as an **accountant/accountent**.

2. The **abolishment/abolishmant** of the tax was very popular.

3. There were **abundent/abundant** supplies.

4. The first **applicant/applicent** got the job.

5. The winner of the prize was unfortunately quite **arrogent/arrogant**.

6. He suffered from a strange **ailment/ailmant**.

7. They formed a useful **agreement/agreemant** over who should do the dishes.

8. Winning the cup was a great **achievement/achievemant**.

9. There was a sound of **distant/distent** drums.

10. The team that had been most **dominant/dominent** won the match.

11. Romy used **disinfectent/disinfectant** to clean the bathroom.

12. The volcano had remained **dormant/dorment** for many years.

13. The **gallent/gallant** knight rode to save the town from the dragon.

14. He moved to a new **continent/continant** to get a new job.

15. They suffered no **disappointment/disappointmant** because they won the game.

Complete these sentences by putting ant or ent correctly on the endings of the words.

16. She was a hardworking, dilig_____ student.

17. The embankm_____ bordered the river.

18. The perfume was very fragr_____.

19. The referee's enforcem_____ of rules in the game was very strict.

20. The environm_____ in the city was much noisier than they were used to.

ant/ent and ancy/ency spellings

21. They only carried essential equipm_____ with them on the trip.

22. The rain never stopped – it was incess_____.

23. Their trip was reli_____ on catching the ferry in time.

24. They ordered an enlargem_____ of the small photo.

25. One day's walk was equival_____ to a two hour run.

Choose the correct spelling in each case.

26. **Accountancy/Accountency** is a well-respected profession.

27. She worked for a top flight **consultancy/consultency** firm.

28. He worked for a successful **agency/agancy**.

29. **Efficiency/Efficiancy** is the key to success.

30. "Is it an **emergency/emergancy**?" asked the operator.

31. The painting's texture had a pleasing **consistency/consistancy**.

32. There was no **urgency/urgancy** in getting to the shops.

33. The musician demonstrated great **proficiency/proficiancy** at playing the tuba.

34. The hotel had only one **vacency/vacancy**.

35. The colours had great **vibrancy/vibrency**.

36. The **tenancy/tenency** agreement ran out and they had to find a new house.

37. America and Australia's **currency/currancy** is the dollar.

38. The **frequency/frequancy** of flights was reduced due to the weather.

39. "His **Excellency/Excellancy**, the King!" shouted the man.

40. They had improved as singers from when they were in their **infancy/infency**.

/40

ie and ei spellings

Fill the gap with either ei or ie to spell the word correctly.

1. They hoped to ach_____ve great success in the competition.

2. The c_____ling needed painting.

3. The fake goods were definitely counterf_____t.

4. Sam bel_____ved that the parcel would arrive tomorrow.

5. The boxer f_____nted and drew his opponent into a false shot.

6. Jagram's h_____ght was 2 metres.

7. They had lots of l_____sure time on holiday.

8. Eating prot_____n is part of a normal diet.

9. The th_____f was caught by the police.

10. She had little pat_____nce with the idea of queuing.

11. He obtained a rec_____pt for the goods he had bought.

12. The thunderstorm was very br_____f. It only lasted 5 minutes.

13. They rec_____ved the parcel with thanks.

14. The b_____ge coloured walls did not meet their approval.

15. None of their n_____ghbours would lend them any food.

16. They went on a for_____gn holiday for the first time.

17. Th_____r house was very cold in the winter.

18. N_____ther Jack nor Diane knew the answer to the puzzle.

19. The book had a very w_____rd storyline.

20. The sailor s_____zed the rope.

ie and ei spellings

Choose the correct spelling in each case.

21. I love taking my **niece/neice** to the park.

22. The park is next to the **feild/field**.

23. I have a mind like a **seive/sieve**.

24. I don't **believe/beleive** it!

25. He was **deceived/decieved** by his friend.

26. They did not **recieve/receive** my letter.

27. Gary cannot **conceive/concieve** of missing his tea.

28. I can hear **sleigh/sliegh** bells.

29. **Veins/Viens** are in our bodies.

30. **Freight/frieght** is carried by trains and ships.

31. They wanted to **forfiet/forfeit** the match.

32. Is that **sufficient/sufficeint**?

33. There are several **species/speceis** of spider.

34. I like studying **science/sceince**.

35. **Either/Iether** we win or lose.

In each of these sentences, an underlined word containing ie or ei is
scrambled. Unscramble the word and spell it correctly in each case.

36. The defence would not lidye. _____

37. The number after seven is gethi. _____

38. She let out a loud hikers when she saw the present. _____

39. The naughty boys often got into micefish. _____

40. There was a dangerous wire on the river, where the water

ran quickly. _____

/40

Adding suffixes to words ending in "fer"

Complete the tables below. Decide whether the "**r**" needs to be doubled before adding the ed or ing ending. The first example has been done as a guide.

Word ending in fer	Add ed
Example: Refer	Referred
1. Prefer	
2. Transfer	
3. Confer	
4. Differ	
5. Infer	
6. Offer	
7. Pilfer	
8. Suffer	
9. Defer	
10. Buffer	

Word ending in fer	Add ing
Example: Refer	Referring
11. Prefer	
12. Transfer	
13. Confer	
14. Differ	
15. Infer	
16. Offer	
17. Pilfer	
18. Suffer	
19. Defer	
20. Buffer	

Adding suffixes to words ending in "fer"

Put the correct ending on these words, so they make sense in these sentences.

21. They could not decide whether it was prefer_____ to stay or go.

22. The prize was not transfer_____, so they could not have money instead of a car.

23. The executives attended an important confer_____ .

24. There was virtually no differ_____ between first and second place.

25. The detective had used the skill of infer_____ to solve the crime.

26. The couple made an offer_____ to charity.

27. There was a large amount of pilfer_____ from the shop.

28. They gave in under suffer_____ as they did not really want to do it.

29. Kiera stood aside, not as much out of defer_____ but out of the knowledge that if she didn't, the man was likely to bump into her.

30. The refer_____ gave a penalty to the away side.

In these sentences, the underlined word ending in "**fer**" has an incorrect suffix. Change it to the correct suffix.

31. The men held <u>differed</u> opinions as to the   _____
correct answer.

32. The matter was <u>referring</u> to the judge.   _____

33. The footballer was <u>transferable</u> to a new team.   _____

34. Many <u>offereds</u> were made to the temple.   _____

35. Ice-cream <u>wafered</u> are really tasty.   _____

36. No-one really <u>suffering</u> from the burden of the   _____
extra homework.

37. They <u>inferring</u> that the problem was not their fault. _____

38. The loan was <u>deferring</u>.   _____

39. The standard of <u>refereed</u> was shocking.   _____

40. The edge of the seat was <u>chamferable</u>.   _____

/40

Antonym fun

Find the antonyms of these words hidden in the wordsearch grid.

big	wide	something	day
come	on	buy	above
full	give	win	grow
up	add	multiply	remember
easy	black	tidy	quick

n	a	r	r	o	w	r	e	l	u	c	t	a	n	t
o	i	i	e	d	m	s	v	o	i	g	l	s	f	d
t	v	g	r	u	n	t	i	d	y	r	i	b	l	y
h	k	a	h	h	j	t	s	s	o	l	i	d	l	r
i	e	m	p	t	y	u	a	t	p	i	o	w	d	h
n	t	w	a	a	s	m	a	l	l	r	f	u	a	p
g	o	k	q	k	e	v	k	y	o	v	e	t	q	i
z	f	s	b	e	l	o	w	x	s	b	r	a	y	e
a	f	i	l	y	l	h	o	r	e	e	c	b	y	p
s	u	b	t	r	a	c	t	p	q	e	c	b	q	n
h	l	w	d	n	l	s	t	p	d	s	k	q	r	a
r	z	o	o	e	a	v	t	n	i	m	h	l	i	n
i	q	r	w	h	i	t	e	g	f	o	r	g	e	t
n	u	d	n	c	h	e	a	v	f	e	s	a	c	n
k	z	d	b	a	e	d	i	v	i	d	e	n	a	z
q	m	e	n	u	v	a	e	i	c	u	m	h	l	t
c	h	e	a	v	i	l	y	u	u	q	e	s	k	q
r	a	n	y	r	u	p	l	y	l	e	x	y	u	v
a	r	m	o	r	i	h	a	p	t	y	a	r	r	i

Semi-colons and colons

The colons are used correctly in these sentences. Is this true or false?

1. You have only one option: leave now, while you can. _____

2. The recipe contained: fruit, biscuits and sugar. _____

3. I can see only one thing: the football pitch. _____

Look at the sentences below. Is the semi-colon used correctly?

Sentence	Can it be joined by a semi-colon? Yes/No
4. Scotland; big mountains, lochs, midges and rain.	
5. I dislike cheese; it tastes strange.	
6. I would like to visit Staffordshire; Stoke!	
7. In the handbag were; scissors, a nail file and her credit card.	
8. I'm not going on holiday this year; it's too expensive!	

Write three sentences of your own using semi-colons.

9. _____

10. _____

11. _____

In these sentences, put in the colon where it is needed.

12. There are two choices at this moment in time run away or give up.

13. This house has everything I need three bedrooms, a fitted kitchen and a loft studio.

14. Paul wanted to know why I didn't answer his text I hadn't received it.

15. These are my favourite foods chips, chips, chips and chips!

16. I bought a lot of meat at the supermarket pork, turkey, chicken and lamb.

Write three sentences of your own using colons.

17. _____

_____

18. _____

_____

/19

19. _____

_____

Apostrophes of omission and possession

Put in the missing apostrophes in these examples.

1. Darren didnt like his new shoes.

2. Samantha wasnt very happy because shed lost her false teeth.

3. Tiffany wasnt late, so the teacher fell over in shock.

4. Anthony couldnt reach the table.

5. April and Chris wouldnt speak to each other.

6. Danielle isnt the smallest in the class, but she looks it.

7. Christian hadnt done his science homework, so his teacher was furious.

8. Natasha couldve won the lottery if shed bought a ticket.

9. Jamie shouldve remembered his book, but hed flushed it down the loo.

10. Nathan hadnt eaten the pies.

11. "Well go to the pictures to see the new James Bond film!" said Leanne to Tara.

12. "Cant I come too?" asked an upset Sarah.

13. Chloe and Harriet didnt grumble when the dinner lady gave them meat pie and custard on the same plate.

14. "Im not very quiet…" said Stacey.

15. "Youll make me sick if you do that!" moaned Adam.

In these examples, you need to change the words to a shortened version with apostrophes. An example is given to you for the first one.

Words	Shortened version word	Words	Shortened version word
can not	can't		
16. should have		17. will not	
18. is not		19. we will	
20. I have		21. you will	
22. they have		23. had not	
24. he had		25. she had	

Apostrophes of omission and possession

> Put the missing apostrophe in each of these sentences.

26. Brendans taste in music was fantastic.

27. Several people commented on how smart Declans shirts were.

28. Kens video camera was the latest model.

29. Willies record shop was the friendliest in Ireland.

30. Chris post on the internet forum was liked by lots of people.

31. Dunkys name was very strange, but it was a real name.

32. No-one understood Lauras handwriting.

33. Where was Davids wallet?

34. Iains name was Scottish or Irish.

35. Everyone was amazed by Gerards artwork.

> In this passage, the writer has attempted to put in apostrophes, but has got some of them wrong, or missed them out. Write out the 10 changes below.

36–45. Jasons' new guitar was very expensive. It had been purchased by his wife Amanda, from a year's savings. The guitars special feature was that it was made from a very rare kind of wood. The woods' special qualities' included making it sound really loud and mellow. Jasons delight at seeing the guitar was great to see. His eyes' lit up as he could not believe that his wife had bought him such a fine thing. Amandas reaction was also one of joy as she liked to see Jason's smiling face. His playing on the guitar was fantastic – his fingers' sped up and down the frets' really quickly – Jasons playing improved greatly as a result of the fine guitar.

36. _____   41. _____

37. _____   42. _____

38. _____   43. _____

39. _____   44. _____

40. _____   45. _____

/45

Commas, question marks and exclamation marks

Put in the commas in these sentences.

1. Emma bought beans cabbages and potatoes for dinner.

2. Despite being very clever Agnes got low marks on the test.

3. Sally Joe and the others emptied the car for their mum.

4. All people have talents but some have more useful talents than others.

5. Priya was a great runner despite getting blisters easily.

6. Unfortunately Joe didn't revise properly.

7. Nadia bought shoes shoes and more shoes in the sale.

8. Fred despite his youth did extremely well in the competition.

9. Betty although she came last enjoyed the marathon run.

10. Whenever she pressed the bell she got a slight electric shock.

Look at the sentences in this table and tick each one to show whether or not the commas are in the correct places. The first one is done for you as an example.

Sentence	Correctly used commas	Incorrectly used commas
Eventually, James got the answer.	✔	
11. Mia ate the biscuits but left the bread.		
12. Laura, ate the bread but she left the biscuits.		
13. Hannah, despite being inexperienced, won the match for the girls.		
14. Cara didn't like her present, despite it being expensive.		
15. Josh, played the bass.		
16. Alan ate cabbage sprouts, and mushrooms.		
17. Isaac's shoes were black, red and gold.		
18. Liam and Tom formed a band, although they couldn't play any instruments.		
19. Kellie, shocked at what she read, gave Mark a telling-off.		
20. Rob, smiled lazily.		

Commas, question marks and exclamation marks

> Put a question mark or exclamation mark in the correct place or places in these sentences.

21. "Why can't I tie this knot properly " muttered Jim.

22. "Look out " warned Anastasia.

23. "Which of these should I wear " asked Danielle.

24. "Land ahoy Over there " screamed the ship's watch.

25. "Matthew – why are you asking Amy " said the teacher.

26. "Ow That hurt " complained Jade.

27. "Is that you, Aaron " asked Shemar.

28. "Don't touch that, James " yelled the PE teacher.

29. "Rebecca Goodness gracious " said her startled sister.

30. "Where is your homework " said the teacher to David.

31. "Brittany No " raged the team manager.

32. "How did you manage to work that out " asked Steven.

33. "Did your photographs come out OK " remarked Kamal.

34. "Watch my fingers " warned Louis.

35. "You're fired " shouted Bill.

36. "Why am I fired " asked Dean.

37. "Because of all the mistakes you made " retorted Bill, angrily.

38. "Why didn't you sack the others who made mistakes "
replied Dean.

39. "Listen to me " screeched Bill.

40. "Why should I listen to someone who shouts all the time "
muttered Dean as he left.

/40

Inverted commas

Put inverted commas around the direct speech in these examples.

1. Pass the ball over here, yelled Domenico.

2. Out! declared the umpire.

3. Ben mused, Where are my toys?

4. I think I know the answer, remarked Sam.

5. That book was amazing, declared Lizzie.

6. Tony! Come here and see this! shouted Phil, excitedly.

7. Wait, said Harry, I think I can hear something.

8. What is it? I hope it's not scary, mumbled Hannah.

9. Maisie – tuck your shirt in! yelled the teacher.

10. Why don't you borrow Abigail's book? suggested Richard.

Is the speech punctuation in the right place in relation to the inverted commas? The first one is done for you as an example.

Speech	Correct punctuation	Incorrect punctuation
"Which one should I choose"? said Gemma		✔
11. "Don't look at me like that!" joked Frances.		
12. "I'm not going to eat that", said Vicky.		
13. "That'll be £2.25, please," said the dinner lady.		
14. "Can you change a five pound note?" asked the pupil.		
15. "Hygiene is very important. Remember that"! ordered the officer.		
16. Amelia shrieked, "It's true – I've won the lottery!"		
17. "I don't want to grow up," sighed Tom.		
18. "Now where did I put that pen"? mumbled Denise.		
19. "Can we have our ball back, please"? asked the boys.		
20. "Remember to bring a change of clothes," commented the instructor.		

Inverted commas

Create some sentences, following the instructions and using inverted commas. The first one has been done as an example. There are lots of possible answers.

Example: Create a sentence that uses an exclamation mark in the speech.

Answer: "Wow!" exclaimed Donna.

21. Create a sentence that has a comma before the final inverted comma.

_____

22. Create a sentence that has a question mark before the final inverted comma.

_____

23. Create a sentence that uses the word **shouted** after the inverted commas.

_____

24. Create a sentence that uses a comma and an exclamation mark in the speech.

_____

25. Create a sentence that uses the word **sad** in the speech.

_____

26. Create a sentence that uses two adjectives in the speech.

_____

27. Create a sentence that uses an adverb in the words after the speech.

_____

28. Create a sentence that uses a comma and a question mark in the speech.

_____

29. Create a sentence that has four words in the speech.

_____

30. Create a sentence that uses the adverb **crazily** after the speech.

_____

/30

Paragraphs

This passage should be split into 10 paragraphs.
Mark where you think each paragraph should start.

1–10.

The first reason why I love folk music is that it is really easy to make with very few
instruments. In the past, people had to make music with whatever they had to hand,
so bones, sticks and stones were early percussion instruments. The next reason why
I like folk music is that it's usually easy to play. Because it was played by ordinary
working people, for their own entertainment, it was not usually complicated, consisting
of perhaps only two or three easy chords. That meant that anyone who had a little
knowledge of an instrument could be a folk musician. Thirdly, the stories that are told
in folk music are fascinating. Many of the songs are really just stories with a tune;
classic stories with timeless storylines, of knights, battles, common folk and rich nobles.
Even if you didn't like the music of some of the songs, the stories would fascinate you.
A different reason why I like folk music is that it is unfashionable at this moment in time.
Who wants to follow the crowd and be the same as everyone else, mindlessly taking in
what the radio and television says that we are supposed to like? Not me, that's for sure.
In contrast to this, I feel that folk music offers tremendous opportunities to find out
about our past. Many songs have been passed down over hundreds of years and
some of the "same" songs exist in slightly different versions all over the country and,
indeed, all over the world. A further reason why I like folk music is that it can be enjoyed
anywhere. It doesn't need expensive microphones and sound equipment (although
they might sometimes help!) and it can be performed in any room, by a small number
of people. Anyone who feels like joining in can add their sound to the music too.
My seventh reason is a personal one – there are many performers and singers whose
voices and choice of songs really appeal to me. Whether it is a distinctive female
voice or a mixture of instruments making a certain sound, there are special sounds
that make me feel good when I hear them. Eighth on my list of reasons is the fact that
attending folk music concerts is really cheap! Because the performers don't need
expensive stage sets and costumes, this means that ticket prices are kept quite low,
which in turn means that fans like me can attend several concerts at a local venue for
the cost of attending one big show in a massive arena. This leads on to my ninth and
penultimate point. When you are at a folk music concert, you will be close to the
people making the music. You will see their fingers playing the instruments and you
will see the glances that the musicians make to each other, the signs that they make
to end the song or to play a solo...and you won't have to look up to see it on a big
video screen. Finally, I realise that folk music is not for everyone, but it does appeal
to all ages and for different reasons – and hopefully will continue to do so, for several
more hundreds, or even thousands, of years!

1

5

10

15

20

25

30

35

Paragraphs

Each paragraph in the passage on page 112 contains a different reason as to why the author likes folk music. Draw lines to match up the paragraph descriptions with the correct paragraph numbers below.

11–20.

Paragraph
First
Second
Third
Fourth
Fifth
Sixth
Seventh
Eighth
Ninth
Tenth

Paragraph descriptions
This paragraph talks about why unfashionable folk music is good.
This paragraph talks about how folk music doesn't need expensive equipment.
This paragraph explains why having easy songs is important.
This paragraph talks about the cost of attending folk concerts.
This paragraph sums up the writer's feelings about folk music.
This paragraph talks about how folk music connects us to the past.
This paragraph talks about stories in folk music.
This paragraph talks about how folk music brings you close to the performers.
This paragraph explains why having few instruments is important.
This paragraph gives personal reasons for liking folk music.

/20

Audience and purpose

Who might be the main audience for these texts?
Circle the most likely answer in each case.

1. A cookery book

   a) Railway enthusiasts

   b) People who like preparing food

   c) Teachers

   d) Children

2. A gothic novel

   a) People who like romance

   b) People who like facts

   c) People who like scary stories

   d) People who like information

3. A GCSE biology text book

   a) Secondary school children

   b) English teachers

   c) Primary school children

   d) Professors of biology

4. A letter of complaint about faulty goods

   a) The government

   b) The police

   c) The manager of the shop where the goods were bought

   d) The advertisers

5. A gadget magazine

   a) Someone who likes trains

   b) Someone who likes phones and cameras

   c) Someone who likes food

   d) Someone who likes astronomy

Audience and purpose

Write a paragraph for each of the following types of audience and purpose.

6–8.

Audience and task	Purpose	Features to include
An e-mail to a friend	To persuade them to go shopping with you	Informal language Two different persuasive techniques

Write your paragraph from the e-mail using the three features shown above.

_____

_____

_____

_____

_____

9–13.

Audience and task	Purpose	Features to include
An opening paragraph from an adventure story for a teenage audience	To entertain	Three exciting verbs Two exaggerated adjectives

Write your paragraph from the adventure story using the five features shown above.

_____

_____

_____

_____

_____

_____

/13

Formal and informal language

Match up the idioms underlined in these sentences with their more formal meanings in each example.

Idiom		More formal meaning
1.	Break a leg in the show tonight!	Fully engaged with work
2.	Be an angel while I'm working.	An emotionally turbulent experience
3.	I don't want this message to fall through the cracks.	On top form
4.	He's tied to his desk.	Gave an exciting performance that everyone enjoyed
5.	Please don't rub salt in my wounds.	Behave well
6.	This week at school has been a roller-coaster ride.	Hard worker
7.	The team were on fire in the semi-final.	Disappear
8.	The band rocked the house.	Calm down
9.	He is a real workhorse.	Good luck
10.	You'd better simmer down or you will be in trouble.	Make the situation worse

The sentences below contain examples of British, American and Australian English slang. Write down the word from the box below that matches the underlined informal words.

Unusual	Rich	Thousand	Failed	Barbecue
Food	Dirty	Friends	Stole	Nothing

11. 'I know **zilch** about cameras. I use my phone.' (American) _____

12. 'He's **loaded**. That's why he can afford fashionable clothes and cars.' _____
(American)

13. 'It's good **tucker** there, especially the desserts.' (Australian) _____

14. 'She's got a great job. Sixty **grand** a year and 150 days' paid leave.' _____
(American)

15. 'You know what happened to Pav? He left his coat on a train with his _____
wallet in it, and someone **nicked** it.' (British)

Formal and informal language

16. 'She's ... strange. Not that weird, just kind of **kooky**.' (American) _____

17. 'I **flunked** my exam, so I'm going to have to re-sit it.' (American) _____

18. 'Their house is so **manky**. I don't think they've cleaned it for ages.' (British) _____

19. 'We're having a **barbie** on Sunday if it's sunny. Fancy it?' (Australian) _____

20. 'Do I know Robbie? Sure! We've been **buddies** for years!' (American) _____

> Read the words and phrases below and the sentences that follow. Choose a literal word or phrase from the A–J list that has the same meaning as the idiom underlined in the sentence. Write A–J in the space provided.

A. were correct

B. make him conceited

C. irritates me

D. write or call

E. fail or succeed

F. ran

G. learning how to work

H. overjoyed

I. bankrupt

J. visit

21. After we won the match, most of the fans were <u>walking on air</u>. _____

22. All this shouting <u>gets on my nerves</u>. _____

23. I hope Carl will <u>stay in touch</u> when he moves to a different town. _____

24. We will <u>sink or swim</u> with this business; there are no other options. _____

25. The men who started up the new company ended up <u>stone broke</u>. _____

26. My little brother is finally <u>getting the hang of</u> his new computer. _____

27. The escaped thieves suddenly <u>hightailed it</u> for the dark backstreets. _____

28. All the flattery and praise began to <u>turn his head</u>. _____

29. I do not like it when people <u>drop in</u> without getting in touch first. _____

30. You <u>hit the nail on the head</u> with your response to the question. _____

/30

Fact and opinion

Look at the statements below. Are they fact or opinion?

1. One plus one equals two. _____

2. One plus one is a really simple sum _____

3. One plus one is an addition sum. _____

4. The coat was red. _____

5. The man had lost his car. _____

6. Port Vale is the best football club in the country. _____

7. It's not a very good website. _____

8. The boy band's album was well-liked. _____

9. I believe that he can win. _____

10. I am the best tennis player. _____

11. I am the world number 1 tennis player at this moment in time, according to the rankings. _____

12. We think Belinda stole the car. _____

13. I didn't have a coat. _____

14. The supermarket is the biggest building in the town. _____

15. You will get cold if you forget your gloves. _____

Fact and opinion

Write two paragraphs about yourself in which you include five facts and five opinions.

16–25. _____

_____

_____

_____

_____

_____

_____

_____

_____

_____

_____

_____

/25

Reading between the lines

Read the passage below and then read between the lines to answer the questions which follow. Take ten minutes to answer the questions after you have read the passage. Circle the correct answer for each question.

Photography is a fascinating hobby. In the days before digital cameras, a photographer would have to be skilled in mixing chemicals and keeping out light so that his negatives weren't ruined. When photography first started, nobody really knew which chemicals worked best and there were several different methods that were used to try to get the perfect picture. Substances such as silver chloride, silver-plated copper and such like were tried with varying degrees of success by men like Henry Fox Talbot and Louis Daguerre. Because such expensive materials were involved, photography was still an experimental hobby for the well-off in society, although there was popular interest in the results.

It wasn't until George Eastman set up the Dry Plate Company in 1880, and produced rolls of film, that photography's popularity really took off. Photography became cheaper and, in 1900, the Kodak box roll film camera made it more accessible because of its lower cost and the fact that up to 100 pictures could be captured on a roll of film.

Experiments in colour photography became more successful in the early part of the 20th century and many travellers helped to create historical records of the time, although many thought that they were just taking holiday snaps to show the folks back home!

Photography hasn't always been about preserving a moment in time – ever since photography started, right up to the present day, there have been people who've sought to deceive the viewer, either with malicious intent or not. There was a trend in Victorian times to fake ghost pictures and, later, many governments and individuals realised the power of a carefully constructed image (especially in wartime) that would tug on people's emotions and get them to change their mind or opinion. The old adage "the camera never lies" is certainly not true and never has been – it can quite often lie! It's been made a lot easier since the development of digital cameras and their phenomenal success. Nowadays, changing photographs has become an art form in itself. There are still many people who think that images shouldn't be doctored, but should remain as they were taken. However, they seem to be fighting a losing battle; if you could remove your age lines and spots and straighten your teeth, you would, wouldn't you?

I certainly would!

1.   What does the word "fascinating" suggest about the writer of this passage?
   a)   He is interested in photography and wants to get the reader to share his enthusiasm.
   b)   He likes using big words.
   c)   He likes using descriptive words.
   d)   Both a) and b)

Reading between the lines

2.   Why does the writer mention Henry Fox Talbot and Louis Daguerre in the first paragraph?
   a)   Because he knows them and wants to show off.
   b)   Because he wants to give evidence to show that he knows his subject.
   c)   Because they invented digital photography.
   d)   Both b) and c)

3.   Which phrase in the first paragraph suggests that photography didn't catch on at first?
   a)   "nobody really knew"
   b)   "varying degrees of success"
   c)   "photography was still an experimental hobby"
   d)   "Photography is a fascinating hobby."

4.   What reasons are suggested in paragraph two for why photography's popularity increased?
   a)   Rolls of film were produced.
   b)   Photography became cheaper.
   c)   A new camera was invented.
   d)   All of the reasons above.

5.   How important is George Eastman to the history of photography, according to paragraph two?
   a)   Very
   b)   Not at all
   c)   A little bit

6.   What does the phrase "although many thought that they were just taking holiday snaps" suggest in paragraph three? It suggests that –
   a)   The early photographers weren't very good.
   b)   The early photographers weren't aware how important their photographs would be.
   c)   The early photographers didn't know what they were doing.
   d)   Both a) and c)

7.   What does the phrase "preserving a moment in time" suggest?
   a)   Photographs can make time stand still.
   b)   Photographs can save a moment for ever.
   c)   Both a) and b)
   d)   Photographs are made of chemicals.

8.   What main idea does the writer suggest in paragraph four?
   a)   That photographs are all unreliable.
   b)   That photographs can't always be trusted as a true record of an event.
   c)   That photographs cause trouble.

9.   Why does the writer use a rhetorical question "you would, wouldn't you?" at the end of paragraph four?
   a)   To get the reader to agree with his point of view.
   b)   To point out how unreliable photographs are.
   c)   To show that photographs shouldn't be changed.
   d)   Both a) and c)

10. Why is the last line in a paragraph of its own?
   a)   To add impact.
   b)   To show a strong personal opinion.
   c)   To trick the reader.
   d)   Both a) and b)

/10

Figurative language

Here are 10 animals that are used in similes. Use the animals to complete the similes.

bat	ox	snail	bird	dog
mule	lamb	bee	eel	mouse

1. He will not change his mind because he is as stubborn as a _____.

2. I cannot go to school, because I feel as sick as a _____.

3. The weightlifter was as strong as an _____.

4. Without her glasses she was as blind as a _____.

5. Omar does so many things – he's as busy as a _____.

6. My laptop has got a virus and is as slow as a _____.

7. Jurgen likes travelling and feeling as free as a_____.

8. Malena was as quiet as a _____.

9. The nurse was as gentle as a _____ with the patient.

10. The untrustworthy man was said to be as slippery as an _____.

Underline all of the metaphors in this passage.
There are 10 to find.

11–20. When I woke up on Monday, my father said that I was a scruffy sheepdog with my long, wavy hair. It was time to get my hair cut. When I gazed at him, he was a zebra, appearing stripy through my overgrown fringe. He was correct – I needed a haircut.

I got out of bed and crossed the desert of the bedroom floor. I quickly washed and made my way downstairs to meet my father who was just about to start up the car. The car's motor was a purring lion as we drove into town to the hairdresser's. The chair in the hairdresser's was a huge tower and it got taller and taller once I sat in it. The hair on the floor was a carpet of fibres beneath my dangling feet. The haircut was soon over and we left the hairdresser's to join the jungle of roads taking us back home.

On the way back, we stopped at the supermarket to get some supplies. There was a big sale going on – we were tiny tadpoles swimming in a sea of fish as we made our way around. Getting out of the supermarket was an awful nightmare too; nothing moved for ages. I hope it's a long time before I'm a long-haired sheepdog again…

Figurative language

Read the sentences below and say whether each one contains a simile, metaphor or personification. Label each simile, metaphor, or personification with S, M, or P.

21. A budding flower was bulging like a wallet stuffed with coins. _____

22. The Atlantic Ocean is a bulging eyeball of water. _____

23. Birds made a playground of the scarecrow's head as it stood in the field. _____

24. The daisies and daffodils danced in the breeze. _____

25. Lexi's bedroom was a garden choked with weeds. _____

26. The trees of the forest gently watched over the lost boy. _____

27. Like a troop of worker ants, the whole team helped set up the goalposts. _____

28. Outside, mist was hanging like old coats between the trees. _____

29. The girl looked around as her class galloped about the room. _____

30. My heart was burning its usual tiny, blue flame. _____

31. The boy was as tall as a giraffe wearing a hat. _____

32. Clouds shed tears of joy over the happy couple. _____

33. Like an arrow, the clever reply made its mark. _____

34. They were as soaked as a drowned tea-bag at the bottom of a teapot. _____

35. The desk jumped across the class. _____

36. The result was as exciting as three birthdays rolled into one. _____

37. She ran like a cheetah. _____

38. The jungle was a blanket of green. _____

39. The desert looked like a blanket of orange. _____

40. Every cloud has a silver lining. _____

/40

Progress report

Record how many questions you got right and the date you completed each test.
This will help you to monitor your progress.

Test 1 /50	**Test 2** /30	**Test 3** /40	**Test 4** /35	**Test 5** /40
Date _____	Date _____	Date _____	Date _____	Date _____

Test 6 /35	**Test 7** /40	**Test 8** Did you find all of the words? If you did it in less than 10 minutes, score yourself 10 marks.	**Test 9** If you got all of the answers in less than 10 minutes, score yourself 10 marks.	**Test 10** /40
Date _____	Date _____	Date _____	Date _____	Date _____

Test 11 /30	**Test 12** /35	**Test 13** /50	**Test 14** /40	**Test 15** /50
Date _____	Date _____	Date _____	Date _____	Date _____

Test 16 /40	**Test 17** /40	**Test 18** /40	**Test 19** /40	**Test 20** Did you find all of the words? If you did it in less than 10 minutes, score yourself 10 marks.
Date _____	Date _____	Date _____	Date _____	Date _____

Test 21 /19	**Test 22** /45	**Test 23** /40	**Test 24** /30	**Test 25** /20
Date _____	Date _____	Date _____	Date _____	Date _____

Test 26 /13	**Test 27** /30	**Test 28** /25	**Test 29** /10	**Test 30** /40
Date _____	Date _____	Date _____	Date _____	Date _____

Answers: English 10-Minute Tests, age 10–11

Test 1
1. boy
2. girl, make-up
3. bands
4. river, banks, town
5. feet
6. Rain, umbrella
7. puppy, chair
8. Canoes, rivers
9. desk
10. answers, class
11. Cars, trains, girls
12. hat
13. Soldiers, monument
14. goldfish
15. boy, sandwiches
16. day
17. happiness
18. intelligence
19. boredom
20. Bravery, quality
21. kindness
22. love
23. courage
24. joy
25. imagination, fear
26. Beauty
27. Revenge
28. loneliness
29. loyalty
30. skill
31–40. Concrete common nouns: riverbank, log, water, clouds, sky. Abstract common nouns: fear, nervousness, threat, anger, sadness
41. boys
42. trip
43. imagination
44. players
45. session
46. entry
47. amazement
48. worry
49. dream
50. coach

Test 2
1. He
2. her
3. We
4. it
5. She
6. It
7. She
8. them
9. them
10. They
11. him
12. it
13. She
14. him
15. They
16. she
17. her
18. She
19. it
20. him
21. them
22. her
23. them
24. him
25. it
26. her
27. it
28. them
29. her
30. us

Test 3
1. ran
2. realise
3. Eating
4. shake
5. spoiled
6. speak
7. eat
8. smiled
9. exploded
10. shouted
11–20. Answers will vary, but each sentence must include an appropriate verb.
21–40. Just a verb: decommission
Just a noun: silliness, sympathy, tablet
Both: run, joke, cry, document, fear, show, question, talk, smell, study, dump
Neither: happy, pretty, clever, blissful, awkwardly

Test 4
1. was running
2. were organising
3. is coming
4. are going
5. are
6. are working
7. was
8. are
9. were
10. is getting
11–20. Correct agreement: 12, 14, 18, 20
Incorrect agreement: 11, 13, 15, 16, 17, 19

21. is
22. were
23. was
24. was
25. is
26. is
27. was
28. is
29. was
30. are
31–35. Answers will vary, but sentences must include is, are, was and were at least once.

Test 5
1. ate
2. performed
3. stood
4. rode
5. had
6. giggled
7. sang
8. invented
9. sat
10. knitted
11. I have found / I found
12. I have studied / I studied
13. I have taught / I taught
14. I have done / I did
15. I have called / I called
16. I have shouted / I shouted
17. I have caught / I caught
18. I have clapped / I clapped
19. I have brought / I brought
20. I have gone / I went
21. The boys <u>were</u> losing at half time.
22. Chuck <u>sang</u> and <u>played</u> guitar in a band.
23. Catherine <u>bought</u> strange clothes.
24. Liam <u>wore</u> fancy dress costumes at parties.
25. Laura rarely <u>asked</u> questions.
26. Isaac smiled a lot, especially when he <u>concentrated</u>.
27. Whitney's loud voice <u>filled</u> the room.
28. Ari <u>walked</u> into the classroom when she <u>was</u> ready.
29. Samuel <u>invested</u> in Internet-based companies.
30. Maisie <u>enjoyed</u> school holidays because she <u>could</u> lie in.
31. He has eaten jambalaya.
32. They have gone to Wales.
33. They have read that magazine.
34. He has lived here for ten months.
35. You have known Michelle for ten years.
36. We have been there for two weeks.
37. I have found my keys.
38. He has drunk too much tea.
39. They have caught the bus.
40. She has gone to Stoke.

Test 6
1. Was the thief caught by the police officer?
2. Were you picked up by your mum?
3. The book is not opened by him.
4. The door is opened by him.
5. A picture is drawn by me.
6. A lot of money is paid by her.
7. You aren't helped by them.
8. Blue shoes are worn by them.
9. The table is set by us.
10. The letter was not written by you.
11. The book is not read.
12. The car is washed.
13. The documents are printed.
14. The food is not eaten.
15. The letter is sent.
16. The litter is thrown away.
17. The shoes are bought.
18. The shop is not closed.
19. The songs are not sung.

20. The window is opened.
21. The race is run.
22. The work is done.
23. The process is activated.
24. The dance is performed.
25. The play is acted.
26. My car was stolen by a thief.
27. Was the letter sent by him?
28. Were they told by you?
29. They were not told by me.
30. The prize wasn't won by her.
31. The song was sung by her.
32. I was hit by someone.
33. He was not let go by them.
34. Their beds were not made by them.
35. The bus was stopped by us.

Test 7
1. dull, dreary
2. Happy
3. Exciting
4. cute
5. tall, imposing
6. expensive
7. Loud
8. skilful
9–15. Answers will vary.
16–25. Answers will vary, but the adjectives used should help to build up a mysterious and spooky mood.
26–35. Answers will vary, but the adjectives used should help to build up a light-hearted and jolly mood.
36. heavier
37. faster
38. biggest
39. noisiest
40. worst

Test 8
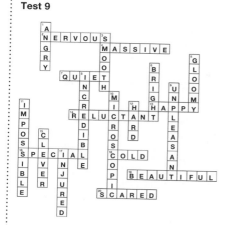

Test 9

125

Test 10

1. quickly
2. amazingly
3. reluctantly
4. lazily
5. Astonishingly
6. Luckily
7. fortunately
8. cleverly
9. crazily
10. cautiously
11–20. Sentences with **ly** adverb: 12, 15, 16, 20; Sentences with **ly** adjective: 11, 13, 14, 17, 18, 19
21–40. Answers will vary.

Test 11

1. We <u>will</u> go to the cinema.
2. We <u>will</u> take part in the sponsored run.
3. They <u>shall</u> win the lottery.
4. They <u>did</u> go swimming.
5. We <u>will</u> stick to our resolutions.
6. She played happily.
7. She sang beautifully.
8. He spoke with her honestly.
9. It was shining strongly.
10. We looked at each other sadly.
11. He played it expertly.
12. They applauded enthusiastically.
13. You dance energetically.
14. He rode dangerously.
15. He visited frequently.
16–30. Many different answers possible. Example given as a guide only.
   Mary walked <u>purposefully</u> towards the shop. It was <u>unfortunately</u> shut, but that didn't stop Mary. She knocked <u>loudly</u> on the door and shouted <u>urgently</u> at the upstairs window. A window <u>slowly</u> opened and a head <u>lazily</u> peered out.
   "Who's that?" said a voice, <u>drowsily</u>. "It's one of your customers!" replied Mary <u>impatiently</u>. "It's past your opening time. Why aren't you open?" There was no reply, but the window was <u>quickly</u> shut and there were sounds of movement going on, before a figure appeared at the shop door. There was the sound of shuffling keys and the lock <u>creakily</u> turned and the door opened.
   "I'm sorry – my alarm didn't go off. Please come in." Mary shrugged her shoulders <u>sharply</u> and strode <u>confidently</u> into the shop.
   "What would you like?" asked the shop assistant <u>politely</u>.
   "Have you got any chocolate biscuits?" said Mary, while fiddling <u>clumsily</u> in her bag for her purse.
   "I'm sorry," replied the assistant <u>hesitantly</u> – "We're a chemist's...."

Test 12

1. beautifully
2. bitterly
3. coyly
4. cleverly
5. Incredibly
6. speedily
7. awkwardly
8. heavily
9. nervously
10. lazily
11–20. Sentences with ly adverb: 11, 12, 15, 16, 18, 19
   Sentences with ly adjective: 13, 14, 17, 20
21. merrily
22. as fast as possible
23. there
24. everywhere
25. at lunchtime
26. usually
27. yesterday
28. last week
29. perhaps
30. definitely
31. sleepily
32. suddenly
33. Immediately
34. hurriedly
35. clumsily

Test 13

1. accept
2. except
3. allowed
4. aloud
5. board
6. bored
7. bail
8. bale
9. break
10. brake
11. canvass
12. canvas
13. Check
14. cheque
15. complemented
16. complimented
17. council
18. counsel
19. dessert
20. desert
21. draught
22. draft
23. duel
24. dual
25. fainted
26. feinted
27. formally
28. formerly
29. Here
30. hear
31. idle
32. idol
33. larva
34. lava
35. lead
36. led
37. lightning
38. lightening
39. lose
40. loose
41. knew
42. new
43. personal
44. personnel
45. plane
46. plain
47. prey
48. pray
49. quiet
50. quite

Test 14

1. thumb
2. doubted
3. feigned
4. gnat
5. knew
6. receipt
7. pseudonym
8. wrapped
9. gnashed
10. wrote
11. bomb
12. climbed
13. combed
14. crumbs
15. limbs
16. numb
17. plumbing
18. doubt
19. indebted
20. thumb
21. knight – someone who might have worn armour, who has the title "Sir"
22. knave – a word implying that someone is of low class or a troublemaker
23. knit – to create material from thread, often with needles
24. knee – the mid-way joint on the leg
25. knot – a tied coil of thread or perhaps rope
26. know – be aware of
27. knock – bang on something
28. knowledge – awareness
29. knife – an item used to cut things
30. knuckle – a finger joint
31–40. Words spelled correctly: 32, 34, 37, 38, 40
   Words spelled incorrectly: 31, 33, 35, 36, 39

Test 15

1–20. Possible answers include:
1. image
2. light
3. hide
4. sleep
5. road
6. courage
7. chilly
8. huge
9. warm
10. gobble
11. construct
12. rush
13. shove
14. purchase
15. see
16. vehicle
17. meadow
18. complain
19. cape
20. trip
21. cracked
22. box
23. arranged
24. cold
25. fly
26. cried
27. brushed
28. tube
29. collect
30. shiny
31–40. Possible answers include:
31. cheap
32. narrow
33. lose
34. alive
35. decrease
36. huge
37. sell
38. short
39. mend
40. close
41. ungrateful
42. disobedient
43. incorrect
44. improper
45. unhealthy
46. illogical
47. impossible
48. unrealistic
49. disorder
50. impolite

Test 16

1. ambitious
2. precious
3. ferocious
4. conscientious
5. facetious
6. fictitious
7. atrocious
8. infectious
9. nutritious
10. fallacious
11. cautious
12. pretentious
13. semi-conscious
14. precocious
15. voracious
16. malicious
17. gracious
18. infectious
19. pugnacious
20. sagacious
21. fictitious
22. contentious
23. scrumptious
24. conscious
25. vexatious
26. essential
27. crucial
28. facial
29. anti-social
30. initial
31. potential
32. preferential
33. martial
34. spatial
35. substantial
36. residential
37. partial
38. torrential
39. beneficial
40. palatial

Test 17

1. accountant
2. abolishment
3. abundant
4. applicant
5. arrogant
6. ailment
7. agreement
8. achievement
9. distant
10. dominant
11. disinfectant
12. dormant
13. gallant
14. continent
15. disappointment
16. diligent
17. embankment
18. fragrant
19. enforcement
20. environment
21. equipment
22. incessant
23. reliant
24. enlargement
25. equivalent
26. Accountancy
27. consultancy
28. agency
29. Efficiency
30. emergency
31. consistency
32. urgency
33. proficiency
34. vacancy
35. vibrancy
36. tenancy
37. currency
38. frequency
39. Excellency
40. infancy

Test 18

1. achieve
2. ceiling
3. counterfeit
4. believed
5. feinted
6. height
7. leisure
8. protein
9. thief
10. patience

11. receipt
12. brief
13. received
14. beige
15. neighbours
16. foreign
17. Their
18. Neither
19. weird
20. seized
21. niece
22. field
23. sieve
24. believe
25. deceived
26. receive
27. conceive
28. sleigh
29. Veins
30. Freight
31. forfeit
32. sufficient
33. species
34. science
35. Either
36. yield
37. eight
38. shriek
39. mischief
40. weir

Test 19

1. Preferred
2. Transferred
3. Conferred
4. Differed
5. Inferred
6. Offered
7. Pilfered
8. Suffered
9. Deferred
10. Buffered
11. Preferring
12. Transferring
13. Conferring
14. Differing
15. Inferring
16. Offering
17. Pilfering
18. Suffering
19. Deferring
20. Buffering
21. preferable
22. transferable
23. conference
24. difference
25. inference
26. offering
27. pilfering
28. sufferance
29. deference
30. referee
31. differing
32. referred
33. transferred
34. offerings
35. wafers
36. suffered
37. inferred
38. deferred
39. refereeing
40. chamfered

Test 20

Test 21

1. True
2. False
3. True
4. No
5. Yes
6. No
7. No
8. Yes

9–11. Possible answers include:
9. The television has broken; I cannot watch the football.
10. My team's playing on Saturday; I hope I can get tickets.
11. I went shopping with my friend; unfortunately, I haven't got any money left.

12. There are two choices at this moment in time: run away or give up.
13. This house has everything I need: three bedrooms, a fitted kitchen and a loft studio.
14. Paul wanted to know why I didn't answer his text: I hadn't received it.
15. These are my favourite foods: chips, chips, chips and chips!
16. I bought a lot of meat at the supermarket: pork, turkey, chicken and lamb.

17–19. Possible answers include:
17. You may be required to bring many things: pens, pencils, art equipment and a sketchpad.
18. I want the following items: an MP3 player, a camera and a new car.
19. I need a helper who can do the following: read Latin, make tea and write clearly.

Test 22

1. didn't
2. wasn't, she'd
3. wasn't
4. couldn't
5. wouldn't
6. isn't
7. hadn't
8. could've, she'd
9. should've, he'd
10. hadn't
11. We'll
12. Can't
13. didn't
14. I'm
15. You'll
16. should've
17. won't
18. isn't
19. we'll
20. I've
21. you'll
22. they've
23. hadn't
24. he'd
25. she'd
26. Brendan's taste in music was fantastic.
27. Several people commented on how smart Declan's shirts were.
28. Ken's video camera was the latest model.
29. Willie's record shop was the friendliest in Ireland.
30. Chris' post on the internet forum was liked by lots of people.
31. Dunky's name was very strange, but it was a real name.
32. No-one understood Laura's handwriting.
33. Where was David's wallet?
34. Iain's name was Scottish or Irish.
35. Everyone was amazed by Gerard's artwork.

36–45. Jason's new guitar was very expensive. It had been purchased by his wife Amanda, from a year's savings. The guitar's special feature was that it was made from a very rare kind of wood. The wood's special qualities included making it sound really loud and mellow. Jason's delight at seeing the guitar was great to see. His eyes lit up as he could not believe that his wife had bought him such a fine thing. Amanda's reaction was also one of joy as she liked to see Jason's smiling face. His playing on the guitar was fantastic – his fingers sped up and down the frets really quickly. Jason's playing improved greatly as a result of the fine guitar.

Test 23

1. Emma bought beans, cabbages and potatoes for dinner.
2. Despite being very clever, Agnes got low marks on the test.
3. Sally, Joe and the others emptied the car for their mum.
4. All people have talents, but some have more useful talents than others.
5. Priya was a great runner, despite getting blisters easily.
6. Unfortunately, Joe didn't revise properly.
7. Nadia bought shoes, shoes and more shoes in the sale.
8. Fred, despite his youth, did extremely well in the competition.
9. Betty, although she came last, enjoyed the marathon run.
10. Whenever she pressed the bell, she got a slight electric shock.

11–20. Sentences with correctly used commas: 13, 14, 17, 18, 19
Sentences with incorrectly used commas: 11, 12, 15, 16, 20

21. "Why can't I tie this knot properly?" muttered Jim.
22. "Look out!" warned Anastasia.
23. "Which of these should I wear?" asked Danielle.
24. "Land ahoy! Over there!" screamed the ship's watch.
25. "Matthew – why are you asking Amy?" said the teacher.
26. "Ow! That hurt!" complained Jade.
27. "Is that you, Aaron?" asked Shemar.
28. "Don't touch that, James!" yelled the PE teacher.
29. "Rebecca! Goodness gracious!" said her startled sister.
30. "Where is your homework?" said the teacher to David.
31. "Brittany! No!" raged the team manager.
32. "How did you manage to work that out?" asked Steven.
33. "Did your photographs come out OK?" remarked Kamal.
34. "Watch my fingers!" warned Louis.
35. "You're fired!" shouted Bill.
36. "Why am I fired?" asked Dean.
37. "Because of all the mistakes you made!" retorted Bill, angrily.
38. "Why didn't you sack the others who made mistakes?" replied Dean.
39. "Listen to me!" screeched Bill.
40. "Why should I listen to someone who shouts all the time?" muttered Dean as he left.

Test 24

1. "Pass the ball over here," yelled Domenico.
2. "Out!" declared the umpire.
3. Ben mused, "Where are my toys?"
4. "I think I know the answer," remarked Sam.
5. "That book was amazing," declared Lizzie.
6. "Tony! Come here and see this!" shouted Phil, excitedly.
7. "Wait," said Harry, "I think I can hear something."
8. "What is it? I hope it's not scary," mumbled Hannah.
9. "Maisie – tuck your shirt in!" yelled the teacher.

10. "Why don't you borrow Abigail's book?" suggested Richard.
11–20. Sentences with correct punctuation: 11, 13, 14, 16, 17, 20
Sentences with incorrect punctuation: 12, 15, 18, 19
21–30. Answers will vary, but inverted commas and other punctuation should be used correctly.

Test 25
1–20. First paragraph (lines 1–3) – This paragraph explains why having few instruments is important.
Second paragraph (lines 3–7) – This paragraph explains why having easy songs is important.
Third paragraph (lines 7–10) – This paragraph talks about stories in folk music.
Fourth paragraph (lines 11–13) – This paragraph talks about why unfashionable folk music is good.
Fifth paragraph (lines 14–17) – This paragraph talks about how folk music connects us to the past.
Sixth paragraph (lines 17–20) – This paragraph talks about how folk music doesn't need expensive equipment.
Seventh paragraph (lines 21–24) – This paragraph gives personal reasons for liking folk music.
Eighth paragraph (lines 24–28) – This paragraph talks about the cost of attending folk concerts.
Ninth paragraph (lines 28–33) – This paragraph talks about how folk music brings you close to the performers.
Tenth paragraph (lines 33–35) – This paragraph sums up the writer's feelings about folk music.

Test 26
1. b   2. c   3. a
4. c   5. b
Many answers possible. Examples given as a guide only as to how they might be done.
6–8. E-mail
Hi Dave – how's things? Doing anything Saturday? A true mate like you would come up town with me. If you don't, I'll tell your brother what you did with his sweets…
9–13. Adventure story
Clare was thirteen, but that didn't mean that she didn't have a taste for exciting, dangerous and breath-stealing activities. She held tightly to the rope as she swung and wobbled in the wind, pressed to the side of the mountain. Rain lashed at her soaked clothes as she dared to look down…

Test 27

Idiom	More formal meaning
1. <u>Break a leg</u> in the show tonight!	Good luck
2. <u>Be an angel</u>, while I'm working.	Behave well
3. I don't want this message to <u>fall through the cracks</u>.	Disappear
4. He's <u>tied to his desk</u>.	Full engaged with work
5. Please don't <u>rub salt in my wounds</u>.	Make the situation worse
6. This week at school has been a <u>roller-coaster ride</u>.	An emotionally turbulent experience
7. The team were <u>on fire</u> in the semi-final.	On top form
8. The band <u>rocked the house</u>.	Gave an exciting performance that everyone enjoyed
9. He is a real <u>workhorse</u>.	Hard worker
10. You'd better <u>simmer down</u> or you will be in trouble.	Calm down

11. Nothing   12. Rich
13. Food   14. Thousand
15. Stole   16. Unusual
17. Failed   18. Dirty
19. Barbecue   20. Friends
21. H   22. C   23. D   24. E
25. I   26. G   27. F   28. B
29. J   30. A

Test 28
1. Fact   2. Opinion
3. Fact   4. Fact
5. Fact   6. Opinion
7. Opinion   8. Opinion
9. Opinion   10. Opinion
11. Fact   12. Opinion
13. Fact   14. Fact
15. Opinion
16–25. Many answers possible. Example provided as guidance of what might be possible.
I am 11 years old and I come from Basingstoke. I own a pair of red trainers. They are size 12. They cost £32.
I don't like eating cheese, but I like yoghurt. My favourite trainers are my red ones. I think that my feet will grow. The trainers were quite expensive.

Test 29
1. a   2. b   3. c   4. d
5. a   6. b   7. c   8. b
9. a   10. d

Test 30
1. mule   2. dog   3. ox
4. bat   5. bee   6. snail
7. bird   8. mouse   9. lamb
10. eel
11–20. When I woke up on Monday, my father said that <u>I was a scruffy sheepdog</u> with my long, wavy hair. It was time to get my hair cut. When I gazed at him, <u>he was a zebra</u>, appearing stripy through my overgrown fringe. He was correct – I needed a haircut.
I got out of bed and crossed the <u>desert of the bedroom floor</u>. I quickly washed and made my way downstairs to meet my father who was just about to start up the car. <u>The car's motor was a purring lion</u> as we drove into town to the hairdresser's. <u>The chair in the hairdresser's was a huge tower</u> and it got taller and taller once I sat in it. <u>The hair on the floor was a carpet of fibres</u> beneath my dangling feet. The haircut was soon over and we left the hairdresser's to join <u>the jungle of roads</u> taking us back home.
On the way back, we stopped at the supermarket to get some supplies. There was a big sale going on – <u>we were tiny tadpoles swimming in a sea of fish</u> as we made our way around. <u>Getting off the supermarket was an awful nightmare</u> too; nothing moved for ages. I hope it's a long time <u>before I'm a long-haired sheepdog</u> again…
21. Simile   22. Metaphor
23. Metaphor   24. Personification
25. Metaphor   26. Personification
27. Simile   28. Simile
29. Metaphor   30. Metaphor
31. Simile   32. Personification
33. Simile   34. Simile
35. Personification 36. Simile
37. Simile   38. Metaphor
39. Simile   40. Metaphor